IN DENMARK
IT COULD NOT HAPPEN

The Flight of the Jews
to Sweden in 1943

Herbert Pundik

gefen בית‖הוצאה לאור גפן
publishing house
JERUSALEM ◆ NEW YORK

Translation from Danish: Anette Mester

Typesetting: Marzel A.S. — Jerusalem.

Cover Design: Studio Paz

The translation of this work has received financial support from The Danish Literature Information Center

Edition 9 8 7 6 5 4

Gefen Publishing House
6 Hatzvi St.
Jerusalem 94386, Israel
972-2-538-0247
orders@gefenpublishing.com

Gefen Books
600 Broadway
Lynbrook, NY 11563, USA
1-516-593-1234
orders@gefenpublishing.com

www.israelbooks.com

Printed in Israel   *Send for our free catalogue*

Library of Congress Cataloging-in-Publication Data
Pundik, Herbert.
[Det kan ikke ske I Danmark. English]
In Denmark it could not happen: The Flight of the Jews to Sweden in 1943/ Herbert Pundik
        p.   cm.
Includes bibliographical references.

ISBN 965 229 176 5

1. Jews—Denmark—Persecutions. 2. Pundik, Herbert. 3. World War, 1939-1945—Jews—Rescue —Denmark. 4. Denmark —Ethnic relations. I. Title.
DS135.D4P8613 1998
948.9'004924—dc21   98-10650
                                                                      CIP

Contents

MY DREAMS AND REALITY

My childhood consisted of dreams and reality. As a rule reality was more fantastic than my dreams. That is probably why I became a journalist.

I was born in Copenhagen in 1927. I was thus eight years old when the Spanish civil war broke out. That is to say, I was too young to sign up as a volunteer in the war against Franco. This, I never got over.

Being a boy in the 1930s was not equally enjoyable for all of us. Some children's parents were unemployed, other children's parents were Jewish.

My father and mother were Jewish. We lived in the same building as Borgbjerg, who was a Social-Democratic minister. That might be why so many unemployed people rang our doorbell. If we offered them food, they would often say that they had just

This picture was taken just a few weeks before the day I was sent home from school with the message that the Germans were after us. I was 16 years old.

had something to eat at Borgbjerg's. In that case they were given money by us instead. Sometimes it was the other way around.

Most of my friends were not allowed to open the door when someone rang the bell in the evening. There was no knowing what these unemployed people might be up to. I was instructed by my parents to go and open the door, so I soon overcame my fear of the strangers waiting on the doormat out there in the dark. On the other hand, I never overcame my resentment of unemployment.

A Life with Caps

My grandfather was a hatter, he made caps. From the age of ten, my father walked around the harbor area selling caps to the dock workers. He never talked much about his childhood, but he would sometimes tell me how nice the dock workers and the sailors on the ships had been to him, when as a child he peddled his caps.

There were eight children in his family, and he was the eldest. My father eventually came to own a villa in the wealthy suburb of Hellerup, as well as a factory, and had a painting by Mønsted on his wall; but throughout his life, I think he felt more at ease among those who wore caps than among those who wore high hats.

My father's childhood stories of the harbor and the ships probably influenced my political attitudes.

There are two sounds that I especially remember from my childhood: Hitler's howling coming over the airwaves from Germany and the hooting of the steamships emanating from the harbor. I liked to imagine that I could tell the difference between the sirens of the "Batory" and the "Pilsudski." These vessels belonged to the Polish-American line and docked in Copenhagen, carrying emigrants on their way to the USA. They played an important role in my childhood.

It was in the early 1930s, and Jews were fleeing from Europe. Especially the Jews who had learned from history and therefore knew that it was better to escape once too often than not.

In my childhood home there were always people on their way from one place to another – on the "Batory" or the "Pilsudski." Jews from Poland or from Germany, clean-shaven Jews who looked like us, and religious men with beards and earlocks, dressed in black.

I didn't know them. As a rule my father brought them home after the service at the synagogue. We were not related to them, but in some way or another we were related anyway. Because they were Jews fleeing. Some of them had to earn money for their passage on the steamships. The easiest way of earning money in Copenhagen was apparently teaching me to read the Bible in Hebrew. My childhood was peopled by a host of temporarily engaged teachers who came and went. And they all started from the beginning with the book of Genesis,

This is my great-grandmother with my father's parents on either side. The picture was taken in 1917, about 10 years after they came to Denmark as poor immigrants escaping from pogroms in Russia.

so I shall never forget that "In the beginning God created the heaven and the earth."

My grandfather came from a small town in Russia called Romny, and there my father was born. The family fled to Denmark in 1905, having survived a pogrom. The pogrom had taken place because the Russian Cossacks were angry that Russia and Tsar Nicolai had lost the war against Japan. This was the fault of the Jews, naturally. But apparently it was not my grandfather's fault, for one Cossack thought it a shame that my grandfather was to be killed. After all, he made such fine fur hats for the Cossacks. The Cossacks therefore hid my grandparents and my father, who was then five years old, in an attic. When the pogrom was over and the Cossacks were resting from the exertion, the family fled to Denmark.

The Flight Motif

The flight motif came to play an important role in my childhood.

I heard about the flight from Russia. And when Hitler came to power in 1933, my mother's parents, German Jews, fled to America – on the "Batory" or the "Pilsudski," of course. One day some large crates arrived in our apartment. They contained items that had remained in my grandparents' home in Germany. There were boy-scout knives and stamp collections in the crates, I remember. They had belonged to my uncles when they were boys.

People pack the strangest things when they have to flee. I experienced it myself later on, when we were about to escape to Sweden in October 1943. It was a Wednesday. And all I put into the suitcase were copies of the magazines *The Home Journal* and *The Family Journal*.

My uncles had no need for the stamps and the knives; they had other things on their mind. One of them was a big game hunter in India, the other was a big game hunter in Africa. They were apparently such big game hunters that they couldn't hunt on the same continent; there simply was not enough game for both of them. That was what the family said. But the real reason may have been that one was older than the other, and that the younger preferred to go hunting by himself.

Pogroms in Russia. The mob drags a Jew away, as soldiers look on. The Russian authorities often let mobs attack Jews to let them blow off steam. Many died and Jewish property was destroyed. The worst period for the Jews was from the 1880s until 1907. Hundreds of thousands fled Russia, the majority across the Atlantic to the USA. My family ended up in Denmark, because they ran out of money while waiting for passage on a ship in the German port of Lübeck.

Within the walls of our own home we felt safe, but I was in no doubt that the grown-up world was out of order. Other children had relatives in the countryside, I had relatives all over the world. Other children's grandparents spoke Danish and came from some known place, my grandfather spoke Yiddish and came from the Ukraine. Hanging on the wall in his home was a green oleograph, on which you saw old Jews with Torah scrolls in their arms. They were fleeing from some Cossacks. To me this was a perfectly normal picture, for at home I was always hearing about people who had fled – or were about to flee. Clouds were beginning to gather over Europe.

There was a blue money box in my grandfather's home. Each Friday the grown-ups would empty their pockets of small change and drop it into the box. I knew what the money was for. It was for buying land in Palestine, so that the Jews might have their own country.

But the thing about Palestine I did not understand until I was somewhat older. Not until 1943. Then it was my turn to flee. I was 16 years old.

And that was the end of my childhood.

THE JEWS GO UNDERGROUND

It was Wednesday morning, September 29, in 1943, at the Metropolitan School in North Copenhagen. We were having a French lesson.

The headmaster entered the classroom, interrupting the lesson. He pointed to me and a couple of my classmates. "Come out into the hall," he said. He spoke it in a kind voice, so apparently we were not in for a scolding. He then

Jews were hidden in this warehouse on Asiatisk Place in Christianshavn in Copenhagen until they could be ferried illegally over to Sweden.

added, "If there are any others among you of Jewish descent, you had better come along." The teacher put some books into his bag and came along.

"We have been warned that persecution of the Jews will soon begin," the headmaster said. "You had better hurry home. The Germans may be here at any moment."

I ran back to my desk and packed my school bag. My classmates were completely silent. We were 16, old enough to understand what was happening. We knew that, at best, it might be a long time before we would see each other again. The boy who shared my desk had just time to hand me his boy-scout compass as a going-away present before I rushed out again.

The thing to do was to get home in a hurry. We lived in East Copenhagen – across from the Langelinie Bridge, which has now been torn down. I got on a streetcar, jumped off at Fridtjof Nansen' Square, and ran across to the newspaper vendor to buy some magazines. A crazy act, considering that the Germans were after me. Who needs newspapers in a situation like that, when it's a matter of getting away in a hurry? Especially popular weekly magazines. But one does not react sensibly to situations of panic.

My parents and siblings were fully dressed for flight: warm winter clothing, a few handbags containing the bare necessities.

My father related that he had been called up at his office by a friend who had attended the morning service at the synagogue on Krystal Street in Copenhagen. The Rabbi had interrupted the service and informed the congregants of the danger threatening them. There were fewer than a hundred people present. He urged everyone to pass the warning on to their friends and acquaintances. No one was to spend the nights to come in his own apartment. They were to seek refuge with Christian friends and acquaintances.

One of those present called my father, who in turn called his old father and his brothers. In the course of a few hours almost all the Jews in Copenhagen had been notified of the German plans.

There was a lot that we had no way of knowing when I came home from school. For instance that two German freighters, the "Donau" and the "Wartheland," were on their way to the Copenhagen harbor to collect the Danish Jews and bring them to concentration camps somewhere down south.

Few photographs were taken during the flight. There were other things to think about.
This is a rare picture. It shows a Jewish woman hiding in a Copenhagen attic. She is
waiting to be brought down to the boat that is to take her to safety in Sweden.

Neither did we know that by this time the Germans had already murdered several million Jews in the extermination camps in Eastern Europe.

We had no way at all of knowing that we would survive the Second World War and the German occupation of Denmark. We hardly knew where we would be spending the next night. We had no idea how we would manage to escape across The Sound to Sweden. Who would help us get in touch with the fishermen along the coast or the members of the resistance movement?

THE TELEPHONES ARE DISCONNECTED

From one hour to the next we had become homeless. We were on the run in our own country, pursued by an occupying power that had declared total war against Europe's Jews. All I owned was a bag with a few kilos of clothing. My stamps and books, from *Tarzan* to *The Collected Comedies of Holberg*, were left behind the shut door, along with my collection of postcards, given to me by two uncles who lived in India and Southwestern Africa.

We were frightened, lost and alone.

My mother gave our apartment key to a neighbor. On my way down I wanted to say goodbye to the girl on the ground floor, whom I never saw again but whom I still imagine might have become my first love. But there was no time.

My father got hold of a taxi. The first stop on our escape route was the suburb of Kongen's Lyngby, where my father had a business acquaintance who would hide us overnight. The following night the German gendarmes came to pick us up. No one answered when they rang the doorbell. They then banged on the door. The neighbors told them we had gone. After that they left.

This scene was repeated from one address to the next. The Jews had gone underground. The German operation was a giant failure. There were approximately 7,000 Jews living in Denmark, but German police succeeded in capturing only about 280 in their homes. Most of them were old people who lived alone, or they were Jews who, for one reason or another, had not been warned in time.

The Germans also succeeded in capturing 190 Jews attempting to escape. Eighty were caught in the attic of a church in the coastal town of Gilleleje. All in all, 477 Jews were seized by the Germans and sent south and from there to Theresienstadt.(1) This was a concentration camp in Czechoslovakia, which had been occupied by the Germans since 1939, before the Second World War broke out.

This picture was taken with a spy camera. It is the only known photograph of Jews being arrested by the German gendarmes. Bystanders were powerless to intervene. The Jews were sent to the German concentration camp, Theresienstadt.

A member of the resistance movement, Erling Foss, has given an account of these events:

> The night of the first and second of October, at 10 p.m., all telephone lines were disconnected, and soon after the operation began. The German gendarmes showed up at any place that had a name plate with a Jewish name on it. In the residential neighborhoods they surrounded the houses...
>
> The expression in people's eyes as they were brought on board the ships was heart-breaking, from what I've heard...
>
> From the various places where the German vehicles were kept, convoys drove off to take up positions at certain points, from which they were then sent out to make arrests. At the same time the telephone service was disconnected to the extent that "Air Defense Warning Service" and "Help" were not functioning. Ritzau's News Bureau was occupied to ensure that their telex machine was not used. The roundup was carried out in very different ways. Some convoys did nothing more than ring the doorbell and when there was no answer, they simply left. In other places, and there were many others, they bashed in the doors or broke the locks... Everywhere Danish-speaking persons accompanied each patrol. The most horrible scenes took place when entire families were abducted... (2)

STATION 3 REPORTS

Here is a detailed police report of the events which took place in Copenhagen that night. It is an excerpt from the police's so-called minute-reports, describing events as were observed by the Danish police:

Friday, October 1:

8 p.m.: Police Inspector Rasmussen (Emergency Unit) reports that 20 large German trucks have left the Free Port in convoy.

9:10 p.m.: The 20 German trucks observed in the Free Port have now proceeded to Ny Carlsberg Street, where they are being manned by German gendarmes.

9:15 p.m.: Police Sergeant Toft, Station 2, reports that 20 German trucks manned by green gendarmes are driving up Strøget. The operation is thought to concern the Jews.

9:30 p.m.: Police Sergeant Toft reports that there are now an estimated 50 trucks. There are also trucks driving down Købmager Street.

9:37 p.m.: Police Inspector Rasmussen reports that all exit roads are now occupied by the Germans, and all vehicles are being stopped and searched.

9:45 p.m.: All telephones have apparently been disconnected.

10:10 p.m.: Station 2 reports that the operation has started in Købmager Street. They have formed a chain across the street, and small, individual groups enter the buildings, returning with civilians. A German major has told a policeman that this is a German affair, and that Danish policemen should not interfere.

Saturday, October 2:

0:55 a.m., The off-duty officer has heard loud engine noises from the direction of Langelinie – Police Officer Buschou reports that the Langelinie pier is lit up, and that there is a lively traffic of vehicles moving towards the steamer at anchor there.

3:15 a.m.: Station 3 reports that guards have been posted along the Langelinie Quay.

8:05 a.m.: Prison warden Kaj Jensen reports he has been informed over the telephone by Horserød camp that the German authorities at this moment are moving the Danish communists. About 150 people, it is indicated.

10:00 a.m.: Three steamers with people arrested by the Germans left Langelinie Quay prior to 10 o'clock, probably going south.

10:24 a.m.: Station 3 reports that the transport vessel "Vaterland" is sailing out of the harbor at this moment. (3)

(The name of the ship was not "Vaterland," as the report has it, but "Wartheland.")

On board were, among others, the brothers Olaf and Johan Grün, Birgit Fischermann and her family, Salomon Katz, his wife and daughter, his parents and many others – on their way to the Theresienstadt concentration camp.

IT CAN'T HAPPEN IN DENMARK

Many Jews feel like the winegrowers on the slopes of the Vesuvius. As long as it only smokes, you can live with the danger. Once the lava is pouring out of the crater, it is often too late to run for safety. The tragedy was that most of those who feared the future and wanted to escape had nowhere to escape to. The countries of the world put a stop to the immigration of refugees in the 30s. This was also the case in Denmark, with very few exceptions.

Hitler's Racial Theories

It was no secret that the Nazi dictator Adolf Hitler sought the lives of the Jews. He declared this policy explicitly and clearly in his book *Mein Kampf*, and he repeated it in a speech in the German Reichstag on January 30, 1939, seven months before the outbreak of World War II.

Hitler considered Jews and gypsies the scum of the earth. They were standing in the way of his idea of establishing a Great Europe under German leadership, inhabited by pure Aryans. Slightly above the Jews were the Slavs, the Russians, and the Poles. According to Hitler's racial theories, these people would be allowed to live on the condition that they submit to the German ruling class. They were to supply the labor force for Hitler's new Europe. But the Jews had to be exterminated. This goal was in part accomplished. In 1941

Deutſche Jugend   Jüdiſche Jugend

Aus dem Geſicht ſpricht die Seele der Raſſe

Nazi propaganda depicted Jews as an inferior race. This cleared the way for the annihilation of six million Jews during World War II. Here is an example of Nazi racial propaganda. On the left: pictures of healthy, blond, young Aryans and übermenschen. On the right: examples of young Jews. The text underscores the message: The face reflects the soul of the race.

Jewish pupils were expelled from German schools. They had to go to schools reserved for Jews. After February 2, 1939, Jewish parents were not allowed to give their children German names. This drawing shows Jewish pupils crying as they are driven from a German school, while the German children smile. The caption: Now we'll have a lovely time in school.

there were 8.7 million Jews in Europe. When the Second World War was over, in May 1945, only 2.5 million were still alive.

We Were Living in a Dream World

The Danish Jews were living in a dream world. We let ourselves be blinded by the fact that our everyday life under the German occupation seemed as ordinary as it was for the non-Jewish part of the Danish population.

The Jewish schools, kindergartens and nursing homes were functioning, and nobody interfered with the services held in the synagogue. There was one exception. Some Danish Nazis threw a firebomb through the fence and onto the synagogue grounds, and in response, young Jews established a private corps of watchmen to protect the synagogue from further attacks. The corps had a direct line to the police station on Nytorv Square to enable them to call for quick assistance.

This was in the fourth year of the war and the third year of occupation. In November 1942, the Germans arrested the Norwegian Jews.

Many had had the chance to escape across the border to neutral Sweden, but they had simply been unable to imagine that the Germans would murder them.

The first news of the Germans' systematic extermination of Jews reached the West from a source in neutral Switzerland in August 1942. The information was met with disbelief, not only by Great Britain and the USA, which were fighting the Germans, but also by the world's Jews. It was the first time in world history that a nation had declared total war on another nation. Wars were fought against armies, not against nations.

Today we are wiser. We have seen a new attempt at genocide in Bosnia. This time we knew; still, the world did not have sufficient will to stop the Serbs.

In 1942 only a few were aware of what was happening in the German extermination camps. It was known that the Germans discriminated against Jews in the countries they were occupying, and that Jews were used as slave laborers. But mass extermination by means of gas chambers? This was beyond belief.

The Germans arrested 530 Norwegian Jews. They were shipped south on board the "Donau." On its way to the Auschwitz extermination camp in Poland, the ship docked at Århus harbor in Denmark. The police knew that the Norwegian Jews were on board, but no one could come to their rescue. A few days after their arrival in Auschwitz most of them were killed in the gas chambers of the death camp. When the Danish Jews' turn came a year later, 500 of the 530 Norwegian Jews had been murdered. Only 30 returned after the war.

September 26, 1943, was the birthday of the Danish King, Christian X. It was celebrated with flowers and Danish flags, and a special service was held at the synagogue in Copenhagen.

A worried verger asked one of the leaders of the Jewish community whether he thought that the Jews would be able to celebrate the approaching New Year as usual. He was reproached with the remark that if he continued to create panic he would be expelled from the synagogue. This was four days before the flight began.

The Jews thought that they could dispel the danger by keeping silent. One reason for this escapism was, of course, that nobody knew how one went about fleeing.

On October 2, the Swedish radio announced that the Swedish government had decided to offer asylum to refugees from Denmark. Until then Swedish goodwill had been lacking. In 1942 the Swedish police had sent Danish refugees back again – often directly into the hands of the Danish police.

THE ESCAPE FAILS

We spent the night with our friends in the suburb of Lyngby, before continuing in the direction of the coast, where we were hoping to obtain passage on a ship across The Sound to Sweden.

From 1943 onwards, to prevent escape across The Sound, small craft were forbidden in the water between Copenhagen and Hundested. This included rowboats and kayaks. At the time of the flight, many boats were illegally returned to the coast. Author Poul Henningsen fled in a rowboat together with the architect Arne Jacobsen. A young civil engineer, Herbert Marcus, was at the oars. The boat was picked up from Bagsværd Lake and carried to the coast by the Falck Rescue Corps.

During the occupation, the Germans gave Falck vehicles special licenses to be on the streets both night and day. Many Jews were transported by Falck.

My parents had no contacts with the resistance movement, but we knew a fisherman in Sletten. We had spent summer vacations at his place. A taxi brought us to the fishing village, where we were given shelter.

The next day we were to go to a certain house situated on a bluff along the coast. We sneaked off in the pre-dawn twilight, afraid of being detected by a German patrol.

This was just what happened to Valdemar Koppel, one of my predecessors as editor of the *Politiken* newspaper, and it also occurred in Sletten, the day after our attempted escape.

Kopel described his capture in a feature article in *Politiken* shortly after our return from asylum in Sweden:

> In heavy rain, gusty wind and darkness we took off, almost groping our way forward... north in the direction of Sletten, where the boat was supposed to be moored in what we hoped was a safe place. I was walking at the rear with a young Copenhagen student who had been involved in the planning, and a fisherman.
>
> We were easy prey. A German car, the first one, drove past without noticing us – we all disappeared behind trees and walls – but shortly afterward a second car came. Or perhaps it was the same car as before which, having lost its way, was returning. This car sealed my fate... There is nothing to add. I was the Gestapo's prisoner.

Along with the student, Koppel was driven to the police station in Helsingør. Somewhere along the way one of the Gestapo men shone his flashlight directly into Koppel's face, asking, "Sind Sie Jude?" (Are you Jewish?). Koppel retained his composure and answered, "Gewiss, sind Sie?" (Certainly, how about you?).

"This counter-question," Koppel writes, "made the Gestapo man sink way back into his corner of the car, horrified at the mere thought of belonging to this race."

Koppel later escaped to Sweden. (4)

Caught in a Trap

We were luckier. At any rate we arrived safely at the large, white villa by the beach, where we were invited to sit down in a spacious living-room. We were to wait until there was room in one of the fishing vessels or rowboats whose owners were willing to risk the trip across The Sound with us.

There were many other refugees in the house. Some had found their way on their own, others were brought there in the course of the night by ambulances belonging to the Falck Rescue Corps. They had been kept hidden in Copenhagen hospitals where the staff had established one of the major gathering places for the Jewish refugees. They were admitted to the hospitals under false names and hidden away in hospital mortuary chapels and boiler rooms. From the hospitals, the Falck men drove the refugees to embarkation points along the coast, from Gilleleje to Holbæk.

That night, the price for getting across was 2,000 Danish kroner per person. This corresponds to 40,000 to 50,000 Danish kroner today (6,000 to 7,000 dollars). Poor refugees were taken across for free. No one was left behind because he or she was unable to pay the "fare," but if you could afford it, it was looked upon favorably if you paid an extra sum into the common fund. The fishermen needed to be paid for risking their lives or their freedom if they ran into a hostile German patrolboat. The following night, Monday, October 4, eight fishing boats loaded to the brim with refugees were seized by the Germans a little north of Sletten, near Snekkersten. The twelve fishermen were sent to the Horserød camp and their ships confiscated. A week later, they were released by a Danish judge with a warning.

Later in the morning it was our turn. We were told to hide on the beach, behind the villa. When the boat arrived, we were to run out onto a bathing pier, where a dinghy would take us the 100 meters to the fishing boat.

It was not our night. At the sound of a boat approaching in the morning twilight, we got ready to run from the house, across the beach and out onto the pier, but the boat sailed past us and moored at another landing. Why, we never discovered.

We wandered back to our summer host who had no idea what to do, either. My father dared not go out, for fear of the German patrols. We were afraid that they were combing the whole area along the coast and searching all houses for refugees. We were caught in a trap, afraid that the Germans were approaching our hiding place.

Perhaps it was our luck that we were so paralyzed. Had we gone to Snekkersten the next day, we might have been seized along with the twelve fishermen and their cargo.

This is one of the rare pictures of the flight. The fishing boat is approaching the Swedish coast.

ROBERT'S VISIT TO DAVID'S HOME

One of my friends, Robert Pedersen, later to become member of parliament for the Social Democratic Party, helped warn the Jews. He was 17 and lived near the Nyboder quarter of Copenhagen. Robert's father was a tailor and a union man. He had heard from Hans Hedtoft, the Social Democratic politician who became prime minister after the war, of the impending action against the Jews.

Robert recounts that his father asked him to comb the whole neighborhood and warn the Jewish families that they had to leave their homes immediately:

> I went from house to house in the streets of the neighborhood: Skt. Pedersstræde, Vestergade, Studiestræde and Pisserenden. Whenever I saw a name plate that indicated a Jewish family, I rang the doorbell and asked to talk to them. Sometimes they did not believe me. But I succeeded in persuading them to pack and come with me to Bispebjerg Hospital which had been turned into a gathering place for Jewish refugees.
>
> I merely turned them over to the receptionist. After that the doctors and nurses took care of them. And then I went back to my neighborhood and collected more Jews. (5)

A Danish Jew, David Sampolinsky, remembers the night when Robert rang the doorbell. Sampolinsky became a veterinarian after the war and now lives in Israel, where he is a well-known scientist.

Sampolinsky's account also says something about the dream world we lived in. We would not believe that the worst could happen:

> We kept on not wanting to believe it. After all, this was a country in which I had grown up, where I had no quarrel with anyone at all. I had had no contact of any kind with the German soldiers. It seemed unreasonable to assume that they, without warning, without any moral right, would arrest and deport citizens of the country. We knew that it was theoretically possible and that it had occurred in other countries,

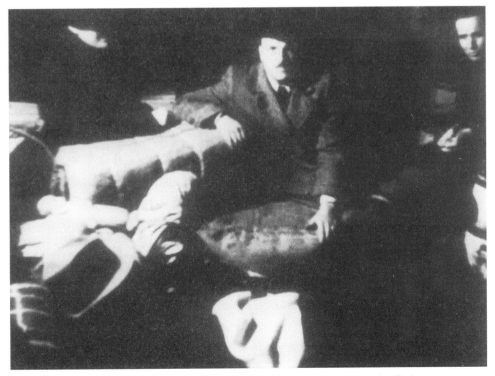

About 2,000 Jews passed through the Copenhagen hospitals during the flight. None were arrested by the Germans. Hundreds of people knew about this escape route, but no one talked. The picture was taken in the Bispebjerg Hospital.

but we could not get used to the thought that it might happen here. Over the past years we had become accustomed to seeing "the green ones" in the streets, where they seemed to behave almost like human beings. Was it conceivable that at the issue of an order they could turn overnight into the worst of predators?

It was the evening before the Jewish New Year when Robert knocked on the door. The Sampolinsky family were together. Since the synagogue had been closed, they held services in their home. When he entered, they interrupted their Hebrew prayers.

David Sampolinsky recounts:

> Toward the end of the service a Danish youth entered the living-room without so much as ringing the bell. He calmly began explaining to us that we ought to break up and leave the apartment immediately... Everyone present had already heard lots of rumors, so his words did not make a great impression on them. They began a discussion among themselves. Then, luckily for us, a surprising change occurred in the young man's behavior.
>
> In a half-choked voice he asked us to leave the house. He had been instructed, he explained, by the local branch of the Social Democratic Party to bring this message to all Jews in the district. He repeatedly begged us to believe him and left the house with tears in his eyes. (7)

Robert's first visit had been to the Sampolinsky family. David was his classmate.

> There was light on the third floor where they lived. I knocked hard on the door. David opened it. I asked to talk to his father, but he said that they were celebrating his sister's wedding and did not wish to be disturbed. I said that what I wanted to discuss with his father was a matter of life or death. Shortly after, he came out into the hallway. I told him that Hedtoft had received a tip-off that the Germans would attempt to arrest the Jews. We did not know whether it would happen

that same night or one of the following nights. They promised to warn as many of the Jewish community as they could get hold of.

Afterwards I called on some families in Studiestræde and Skt. Pedersstræde. The strange thing was that people would not believe me. In one family the man said that he would call the Chief Rabbi to have the warning confirmed. But since his phone was probably bugged by the Germans, I threatened him to keep him from doing so. If he did, I would shoot him. Which was ridiculous, as I did not have a gun.

But his wife saved the situation. She posed the very sensible question: Why would I have come to warn them, if there wasn't something to it?

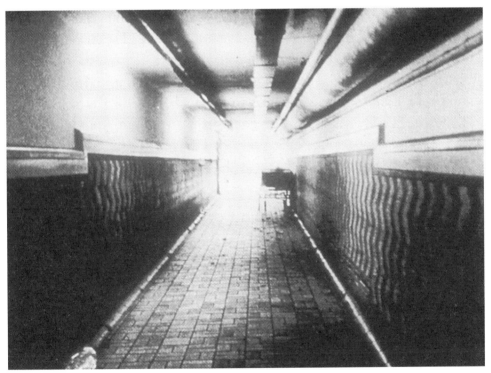

Basement at Bispebjerg Hospital in Copenhagen
where Jews went into hiding.

I drove the Jews to Bispebjerg Hospital, where they were registered as patients and hidden in the basement.

I remember an episode involving an old lady. She was 90 years old, and I had driven her out to the hospital. Here she became very upset. I could not understand what she said, because in her agitation she spoke Yiddish. A Jewish doctor told me that the lady was upset because she had forgotten the cerements she had prepared for her own funeral. She could not leave for Sweden without her last and final dress.

At that moment Urban Hansen came by. He was the one in charge of transporting the Jews to the hospitals and later became the Lord Mayor of Copenhagen. He was a man with a fierce temperament and, when he heard what was wrong, said: We are saving people, not clothing. You will not be allowed to go back to her apartment.

I did so nevertheless. I had to return to the neighborhood anyway to collect more Jews. How they would continue onward to Sweden, I did not know. Others would see to that at Bispebjerg Hospital. (5)

Robert Pedersen's and David Sampolinsky's stories are typical of the atmosphere of those days. Many Jews would not believe the warnings.

The many Danes who went from house to house to warn the Jews and help them go underground sometimes had to visit the Jewish families two or three times before they were taken seriously.

OLSEN AND ABRAHAMOWITZ

Two groups played a prominent role in the resistance movement against the German occupation: priests and doctors.

Not only was physical courage required to enter into the illegal activities of the resistance movement, you also had to have connections.

In the first years of the occupation, the resistance movement was not a broad, popular organization. It was a small, solid group of silent men and women. They knew that talking could cost them their lives. For many Danes it was difficult to get into contact with the underground. Often people became involved with the movement by a mere chance.

Ole Lippmann was one of the first members of the resistance group and in time became one of the most important. He was chief of secret communications with England and in charge of the agents who were dropped by parachute over Denmark by English and American planes. They came to help organize and train Danes for sabotage and other underground work.

He recounts how it was often a blind chance that determined whether a person became involved in underground activities. The following situation is a construct. The names are fictitious, but the course of events is very typical for the occupation:

The Olsen family lived in the same house as the Abrahamowitz family. The men would enjoy an occasional drink of beer together after hours. Their wives had coffee together every morning. Sometimes they would eat supper together. The Abrahamowitz family observed the Jewish dietary laws, so they did not eat pork.

One day Olsen hears rumors at his workplace that the Germans are planning to arrest the Danish Jews. He calls on the Abrahamowitz family the same evening and invites them to spend the night in his apartment. During the night the Gestapo arrive. They knock on the door to the Abrahamowitz's apartment, but leave when no one opens the door.

At his workplace Olsen recounts the events of the night and the visit by the Gestapo. One of his colleagues knows somebody who knows somebody who might be able to help. That same evening a stranger shows up at the Olsen's. He tells them that a little later someone will be coming for the Abrahamowitzes. They are picked up, driven to the Copenhagen harbor and hidden in an apartment where they meet other fugitive Jews. Everyone is frightened. Nobody tells them what is going to happen. Later in the night a young girl enters, wearing a red beret. She says there is room for four on the

Fisherman Jens Møller from Gilleleje. He was ship's boy on his father's fishing boat. "Two or three days went by before the Jews could get across. I ran back and forth to the harbor all day to see if there was room for them." (6)

next boat to Sweden. Abrahamowitz and his wife follow her and disappear into the darkness.

But this is not the end of the Olsen story, reports Ole Lippmann:

> One day the stranger who picked up the Abrahamowitz family shows up and asks for the key to the Abrahamowitz's empty apartment. He gets it and changes the name plate. It now says Kurt Jensen on the door.
>
> Strangers come and go in the apartment. Some stay a couple of days, others longer. They are all called Kurt Jensen. It says so on their ID-cards, so it must be true. In the evening when the apartment is empty, Mrs. Olsen goes in there and straightens up a bit. They all look so tired – and hungry – so she also puts out some food. From time to time Olsen has a chat with the underground people. He starts helping them, first by delivering letters around town. Slowly they begin to trust him, and he becomes more and more involved in the fight against the Germans. It started with his lending a hand to his Jewish neighbor one night in October. Olsen is now a saboteur. (8)

A Spontaneous Act

The story of Olsen shows two things: one is that there was no underground organization standing ready to save the Danish Jews in October 1943. The rescue operation was an altogether spontaneous act, completely improvised.

The Olsens all over the country – like their Jewish compatriots – were facing a problem. In the beginning they acted without any plan whatsoever, without any central leadership that could issue orders, without any capital to finance the rescue operations. They helped their Jewish neighbors, their colleagues at work and often total strangers as well.

The German action against the Jews had aroused anger in many Danes. Helping the Jews was also a demonstration against the German occupation.

One month earlier, on August 29, 1943, the government and the parliament had resigned. King Christian X had shut himself up in Amalienborg Castle.

The Danish army had been interned by the Germans. The Danish fleet had sunk its ships or taken them to Sweden to prevent their being seized by the Germans and used in the fight against Great Britain and the USA.

The Danish resistance had attained its preliminary political goal – the reversal of the policy of collaboration that had characterized the relationship between Denmark and Germany since April 9, 1940, when Denmark was occupied.

The Germans had practically declared war against the Danish population. When the Germans took action against the Jews one month later, many Danes responded to this German declaration of war by rescuing Jews from the German police patrols.

The Danish people's patience with the Germans had run out in 1943. The picture is from Odense, a city in revolt.

Twenty People Knew We Were Escaping

What the Olsen story also shows is that the help he gave the Abrahamowitz family was only the beginning of his work for the resistance movement. Many followed Olsen's example and continued their underground activities after the task of rescuing the Jews had been completed.

There is no knowing exactly how many participated in the rescue, but there were certainly tens of thousands.

It took my family four days to get from our home in East Copenhagen to the Swedish coast. In the course of those days we came in contact with more than twenty people who knew that we were escaping. They helped us in various ways. There was the family in Lyngby where we spent the night; the taxi driver who took us there; the fisherman and his wife with whom we stayed; old Nicolaisen who found us hiding in the fishing hut in Sletten, not knowing how to get any further; the fisherman who finally took us across The Sound; not to mention the wives who did not object to their men helping us on our dangerous journey.

All of them knew that we were escaping from the Germans. Only a few talked too much. Even fewer refused to help. They acted as if they had no choice.

The poet Halfdan Rasmussen wrote of this generation:

> We were so young. And our choice
> was between death and violence.
> We had no faith for sale.
> And did not ask for recompense.
>
> Our faith was pure. We had to fight
> if the world was to continue.
> There was but one life. It had to do with us
> and all that we held true. (9)

THE HOSPITALS GO INTO ACTION

Bispebjerg Hospital was where Robert Pedersen and many others brought the Jews they had managed to warn, and who had nowhere else to hide.

Why did a hospital become the gathering place for Jews who had to go underground? The relationship of trust between doctors and patients played a role.

In the last half of September 1943, the air was thick with rumors of an impending action against the Jews. It was natural that they should talk to their doctors of their worries. After all, doctors were bound by a vow of silence. Many doctors had connections to the resistance movement, and they were obligated to help people in trouble and to guard secrets.

At times they were called to an address where they would find a wounded member of the resistance who had been shot by the Germans, or had broken a leg while trying to escape from German pursuers.

The doctors knew more of the Germans' brutality than did many other Danes.

Doctor Steffen Lund tells about... the terrible days and nights (around the 29th of August). One would sit by helplessly looking at young, innocent people who had been killed by a bunch of insane brutes running around in the dark shooting wildly...

The hatred for the Germans that had existed at the hospitals throughout the occupation rose a good degree or two during those days...

An elderly, trustworthy ambulance driver told, for instance, that he had been driving across Knippels Bridge when an old lady came walking quietly and peacefully along the pavement. Suddenly he saw a German soldier raise his gun, aim it for no reason at all at the unsuspecting lady and shoot her down. She died shortly after being admitted to the Sundby Hospital.

After the 29th of August came the action against the Jews.

Steffen Lund tells of his consternation and dismay. "We didn't think it could happen in Denmark."

His naiveté was as profound as David Sampolinsky's. Their reactions were almost identical, word for word:

> Even though you had seen actions taken against Jews in all the other countries occupied by the Germans, the thought of a particular group of Danish citizens being persecuted seemed so remote that no Dane really believed such medieval, bestial acts could take place right in our midst...
>
> In those days, before the persecutions set in, we decided that the hospitals would do what they could to help...
>
> It was a natural task for the hospitals to open their gates and try to hide the Jews...
>
> The Jews were admitted under false names to all the hospitals of the city... Thus it was of no avail if the Germans came and checked our records, for there was not a single Jew registered... It was best to hide the Jews in large institutions, in case the death penalty should be issued against those who were hiding them, as happened in other countries. In a large hospital it would be difficult to find the one who was responsible. No one, of course, could refuse to admit a patient called Hansen or Jensen – even if they did not look quite Aryan. (10)

HIDDEN AWAY IN PARKS AND WOODS

Some Jews had fled without finding shelter with non-Jewish Danes. Some stayed in the parks around Copenhagen, especially Ørsted Park. At night they sneaked across the street to the Municipal Hospital where they were given food.

There were also a number of Jews who had hidden themselves in the woods near Copenhagen. The Copenhagen hospitals contacted the University Rifles Club, which placed 200 volunteers at their disposal. These marksmen combed all the woods in the whole country. The Jews they found were smuggled into the Copenhagen hospitals, and from there they were transported to Sweden.

Professor Ole Secher was a medical student in 1943. He organized, among other things, an escape route that started in Nykøbing Falster.

In a forest near the town of Herfølge the marksmen found 13 Jews. They had been hiding for a week, living on nothing but the beets they found in the fields at night.

The Copenhagen Hospitals Saved 2,000 Jews

After some days of improvisation the work was systematized. Every morning representatives of all the hospitals in Copenhagen met to report on the number of Jews being hidden, in order to organize their transportation across The Sound. Not all of this proceeded without moments of danger.

One time, Steffen Lund recounts, Bispebjerg Hospital was surrounded by the Germans. On that night 200 Jews were hidden in the hospital. It was feared that the Germans would begin their search early the next day, so the refugees had to be moved. At nine o'clock in the morning a funeral procession rolled out of the chapel. In the rented cars, which the Germans did not check, were 200 Jews on their way to Sweden.

Another day 100 Jews were to gather at Blegdams Hospital. They came from many different hide-outs around Copenhagen. Each was told to show up with a small handbag and a bouquet of flowers, as if they were visiting a patient. From the hospital entrance they were directed to the chapel, from which yet another funeral procession left shortly thereafter.

All in all the Copenhagen hospitals managed to save about 2,000 Jews, sending them to Sweden. The illegal routes to Sweden departed from 27 different places on Zealand, from Udsholdt in the north to Hesnæs in the south. The rescue operation lasted two weeks. None of the transports was seized by the Germans. No one was hurt, neither refugees nor helpers.

Once things almost went wrong. On the 10th of October a message was delivered to Bispebjerg Hospital that a ship was to leave Strøby, ten kilometers south of the town of Køge, that same night. There was room for 180 passengers.

Some hours later, a convoy left from the back entrance of the hospital. It consisted of rented cars, moving vans and some Falck ambulances. One of them had 17 Jews packed into it. All the drivers were highly trusted men. The

The beech forest at Gjorslev on the peninsula of Stevns was an important embarkation point. The refugees hid in the woods until contact was established with the illegal escape ship. They were then rowed out from the bathing pier. (11)

hospital had acquired a list of reliable cab drivers who did not sympathize with the Germans.

The transport reached Strøby safely, but this fact was not communicated to the Bispebjerg Hospital headquarters. The usual report verifying that all was well was not received.

A Falck inspector drove off to find out what had happened, but he did not report back either. Then two police officers who had volunteered to help went to investigate. Their uniforms and police badges protected them to a certain extent from German pursuit.

A while later there was a report from the policemen. The whole operation had nearly failed.

The ship that was to bring the Jews to Sweden had sent signals to the help on land. But the signal lights had been answered by machine gun fire. There had been a German patrol ship out there in the darkness. Several hundred people, refugees and helpers, had to flee from the beach into the forest. The German ship vanished into the night.

A convoy of people from the Civil Defence, called CDs, helped evacuate the Jews from Strøby to Fanefjord on the island of Møn. From here another ship brought them across the sea to safety in Sweden.

We Thought We Were All Alone in the World

We were sitting in our hiding place with the fisherman in Sletten, cut off from the rest of the world. The fisherman had gone down to the harbor to find out whether anyone wanted to sail across The Sound.

He returned without having accomplished his objective. Unfortunately he did not know the doctor in Snekkersten, Jørgen Gersfelt, nor the innkeeper Henry Thomsen. He could not know that a few kilometers from Sletten there was a lively traffic of Jews in those days. We thought we were all alone in the world.

The Gilleleje train brought hundreds of Jewish refugees from Hillerød to the coast. The Germans could easily have stopped and inspected the train. This did not happen.

Jørgen Gersfelt wrote about his experiences after the war. (11)

Hundreds of Jews came on the coastal railway from Copenhagen in the hopes of escaping. They were received at the station by volunteers who hid them in empty summer houses. Gersfelt's friends and aquaintances had asked him to keep an eye on their houses over the winter and had given him the keys. The Gersfelt home became a vital center. He hid Jews. When they were about to cross The Sound, he picked them up in his doctor's car which had a special license to drive at night in spite of the curfew. The fishermen came to him with information about how many they could bring over during the night and what it would cost. Gersfelt composed the passenger lists, so that the refugees who could afford it paid for the poor refugees. He gave sleeping medicine to the young children, so that they would not cry and warn the Germans during the passage, and he gave sedative injections to the adults. The men were often the most frightened, he recounts.

There was good reason to be afraid. The passage could be dangerous, especially in the beginning, when the journey was by rowboat. At best it would take four or five hours, depending on the weather conditions and the currents. The fishermen did the rowing, but the going was hard, and other volunteers lent a hand. Some of the boats were heavy. It was an almost superhuman task to row them across fully loaded – as they were – with refugees.

Gersfelt tells of a feat which to him is one of the finest examples of the Danish will to help their compatriots in need. A retired mailman, a 70-year-old gardener and a barber helped a fisherman row across. The journey lasted all night. The only one with any experience in handling the oars was the fisherman.

THERE WERE ALSO TRAGEDIES

One night Gersfelt drove an old Jewish couple from Skovvej in Snekkersten to Tibberup Hills, where the rowboat and the fisherman were waiting. They

Some Jews were captured by German gendarmes who were checking automobile traffic on the Coast Road. "We were asked if we were Jews, and we had to answer yes," tells Johan Grün. "We were driven to Langelinie in German military trucks." The picture is from the film, "One Day in October," directed by Kenneth Madsen.

were frightened and worried, and their premonitions were confirmed. The boat capsized off the Swedish coast. The man and the fisherman drowned, the wife survived.

One man was in such despair that he cut the throats of his wife and their two children. He had no way of knowing that the rowboat which was to bring the family to safety was already waiting for them on the shore.

There were comical episodes as well. Gersfelt tells of a couple of volunteers who were stopped by a Danish policeman while carrying a rowboat from land out to the shore.

One of them stuck a gun into the policeman's belly and asked him if he was a good Dane. Well yes, he certainly was, and helped carry the boat the rest of the way.

Everyone was frightened during the flight. No one had any way of knowing that the Germans would not do their utmost to capture us. The picture shows a young Jew on his way below deck on a fishing boat.

Thomsen, the keeper of the Snekkersten Inn – who used to be a fisherman – and his cook were rowing across one night. Along the way the drain plug was knocked out by a rock, and the water came pouring in. The cook had to spend the rest of the journey with his finger in the hole.

The Danish police often helped. Once an informer rang up to tell them that a group of Jews was about to escape. The police arrived with the "paddy wagon," arrested the Jews, drove them to Snekkersten and told them to look up Thomsen at the inn.

Another time a group of Jews was arrested by the Danish police and brought before the court in Helsingør. The Germans heard about it and showed up in court, but the judge ordered the doors closed, and the Germans were forced to wait outside the courtroom.

When the sentence had been delivered, the Germans demanded that the Jews be handed over to them. They were told that the Jews had been transported to the county jail to serve their sentence. When the Germans arrived at the jail they were told that the Jews had escaped en route. At that moment they were already on their way across The Sound in one of the Coast Guard speedboats.

While all of this was happening around us, we sat waiting in Sletten.

THERE IS A KNOCK AT THE DOOR

At the same time an elderly man, leaning on his cane because he had trouble walking, went from house to house along the coast. He asked whether anyone had seen the Pundik family. His name was P. Nicolaisen and he was my father's business acquaintance. The man who had put us up that first night in Lyngby had informed him that we were somewhere along the coast. Neither of them knew where. In his desperation Nicolaisen had decided to search through all the fishing villages south of Helsingør on his own, house by house.

It is 10 kilometers from Helsingør to Sletten. He knocked on every door along the way. The odds were poor, but he would never have found peace if he had not done his best to save us from the Germans.

In the late afternoon there was a knock on our door. We rushed into our hiding places: under the beds, in a closet, behind a door.

"My name is Nicolaisen," a voice said. "I am looking for the Pundik family. Have you seen them at all?"

Our host, the fisherman, said no. Everyone was afraid of informers along the coast. "Gestapo-Juhl" and his men were operating in Helsingør. Gestapo-Juhl was a Danish-speaking man from southern Jutland.

My father recognized the voice and let himself be known. Nicolaisen came in, and we emerged from our hiding places. The same night a car with a doctor's emblem arrived. Perhaps the driver was Gersfelt, he did not introduce himself.

By the back roads, he drove us to Ålsgårde where we were installed in Nicolaisen's house. It was situated on the land side of the Strand Road. On the other side was an open beach.

The rest of the story of our escape is undramatic. Nicolaisen found a fisherman who was willing to sail us across, and the following night we crept across the Strand Road and down to the beach where the fisherman was waiting with a dinghy. His boat was 100 meters further out.

The End of Four Days' Flight

I remember the last glimpse I caught of the coast before being ordered below. On the beach Nicolaisen and his wife and the fisherman's wife were kneeling in the morning twilight. Their folded hands were lifted toward the sky.

I remember that I looked at my watch when the engine started. Thirty-seven minutes later we passed into Swedish territorial waters. A Swedish patrol boat hailed us, and we were allowed to come up on deck. "Welcome," the Swedish sailors called out. One of our fellow passengers said a prayer in Hebrew in a loud voice, a prayer thanking the Lord for salvation. The rest of us said "Amen."

The escape had lasted four days. I do not really remember our first days in Malmø, Sweden. My parents rented a small apartment. My father began looking for work. Just a week after I had emptied my desk at the Metropolitan School, I was in a classroom again, at the Realskolan in Malmø. I was surrounded by Swedish pupils who could not understand why I didn't feel like going dancing with them on Saturday night.

The poet Otto Gelsted also had to flee during those October nights. He has written a poem titled "The Flight" about his experiences:

The Flight

Against the stars a swaying mast
without a single light,
a ship with human cargo
moving through the night.

Jews fleeing across the Sound
in October, dark and cold,
huddled together on the rolling deck
and packed into the hold.

Only a nutshell in the sea of blood
and horror, a vessel afloat,
the hellish sea created by Hitler,
only a fishing boat.

Running away from terror and death,
from violence and torture,
with German patrol boats along the coast
waiting to make a capture.

And leaning against the railing I thought
of the ships that had sailed away,
from Oslo and Copenhagen, with Jews on board
destined for Germany.

I thought of the woman who chose to leap
overboard with her child,
rather than see it trod under Hitler's heel
suffering and defiled.

Those ships were named Donau and Vaterland,
and never shall any name
be carried from harbor to harbor
with greater disgrace and shame. (12)

THE SECRET WAY

All the Jews tried to flee the country as soon as they heard of the danger of arrest, except for a handful who had various reasons for staying in Denmark. One of them was Robert's classmate, David Sampolinsky.

Foreign Jews in Vestre Prison

David had sworn that he would be the last Jew to leave the country. In his uniform, as a member of the civil defence organization, he fine-combed Copenhagen to make sure that no Jews had been forgotten. During that time, he lived illegally at the Municipal Hospital.

One day he was told that a small group of foreign Jews was locked up in Vestre Prison. They had been arrested by the Danish police either for entering the country without a permit, or because their residence permit had expired. David went out to the prison. He asked the warden to release them, as they might otherwise fall into the hands of the Germans, but the warden wanted to see an order from above.

David recounts that he bicycled out to the home of the former Prime Minister, Vilhelm Buhl, and asked to be allowed to speak to the Social Democratic politician. But when Buhl heard what it was about, he said that he neither would nor could interfere in the matter.

David left in despair. He recalls that for reasons of safety he hid in a gateway until the coast was clear and no Germans were in sight. From his hiding place he saw Buhl come out and take off on his bicycle. The next day he was told that the young Jews had been released and sent to Sweden. Shortly thereafter David himself went there too.

Incidentally, this is one of the few positive things to be said of Buhl's behavior during the occupation. From first to last, he was opposed to the resistance movement's fight against the German occupation.

Glück, who tried to escape by hiding under a railroad car, ended up in the Auschwitz death camp. He survived and now lives in Israel. The picture was taken when Glück visited Denmark after the war.

Underneath Freight Cars Leaving Denmark

Another young Jew who did not escape right away was Hermann Waldmann. In Israel he took the name of Uri Yaari.

He had come from Germany to Denmark as a boy in 1938. Conditions had grown steadily worse for the Jews in Germany. Young people were thrown out of their jobs as apprentices and dismissed from schools and universities. Non-Jews were not allowed to patronize Jewish shops. And Jews were punished if they did not wear the yellow Jewish star in plain sight. Many young Jews were sent to Denmark by their anxious parents to learn agriculture on Danish farms. From here they were to proceed to Palestine.

The German occupation trapped many who had not moved on in time. Hermann was one of them. Together with some friends he organized one of the most dramatic attempts at escape from Denmark.

Their aim was to get through occupied Europe and into a neutral country, Switzerland or Turkey, not at war with the Germans. From here Hermann and his Jewish friends hoped to continue to Palestine.

Their method of escaping was as original as it was adventurous.

The young farming apprentices had discovered that they could crawl and hide underneath freight cars leaving the country. There was just enough room for one man and his food and drink.

Hermann's group was well trained. Before they set out on their expeditions through Europe, they trained at home: first in the forests, and later on by entering Danish and German military areas without being detected. Finally they trained by getting across the Danish-German border into southern Schleswig undiscovered.

So it was possible. The Germans were not aware of the hiding place underneath the railroad cars.

Hermann was the first to test the method. He found a freight car going south from the Odense railway station and placed himself on the undercarriage between the wheels, right above the rails. In this way he reached Holland without being discovered. Here he found another freight train going to

Denmark, and returned in the same manner. Within twenty-four hours he was in Fredericia in Denmark.

The Method Worked

One of his friends, Bertl, made the next trip. He got as far as Sofia in Bulgaria. He could have gotten away, for Bulgaria was a semi-neutral country from which it was easy to get to Turkey and then on to Palestine. But Bertl had promised his friends to return to Denmark and report.

He found a train from Sofia going north through Europe. In Hamburg he was discovered by a German railwayman who denounced him. He was sent to the Auschwitz death camp, where he met Alfred, one of his friends from Denmark, who had also attempted the trip but had been caught at the Swiss border.

Bertl was murdered in Auschwitz, but Alfred survived and after the war settled in Israel with a wife and a lot of cats. He came to feel sympathy for cats during his long stay in the death camp, where the German guards had amused themselves by torturing cats.

In an interview with Johannes Christiansen, Alfred recounts:

> After half a year's training on several trips far down into Germany, during which no accidents occurred, the group was ready to implement its final plan of reaching Palestine.
>
> A friend and I crept into a freight car and hid in a crate. The car was sealed and the journey began.
>
> For more than a week we lived like moles in the dark... We ran out of water... Soon we had only oatmeal and a bit of butter left. Our mucous membranes dried up... Our feet were swollen so that we couldn't get our boots off... Nature had to be relieved in the crate, of course... We were lying on the straw trying to sleep... Thirst was burning like fire in our bodies. My friend became delirious, he ran a high temperature.
>
> We heard someone rummaging outside; the door of the freight car was unlocked. A ray of sun played on the ceiling... the door was being

opened. I put my hand across my friend's mouth. His whole body was shaking.

Were they in Switzerland or in Germany? Had they been detected? The door slammed shut. Then it was opened again and on the platform German gendarmes in green uniforms were standing in a semi-circle.

One of the soldiers said that he was the one who had discovered them. When he had opened the door of the freight car, he had noticed an empty box of Danish oatmeal on the floor, which they had forgotten to hide.

They were questioned and brought to a prison where their identity cards were stamped "to be transferred to Auschwitz." (13)

AUSCHWITZ HAS GAS CHAMBERS

"We did not know what Auschwitz was," Alfred recounts. But one night a young man was kicked into their cell. His face was swollen, one eye was crushed. The fingers on both hands were broken. He was a Polish student, arrested for having been a member of an underground group.

"When we told him that we were being sent to Auschwitz, he stared at us in horror," Alfred relates.

"Auschwitz is an extermination camp. In Auschwitz there are gas chambers where thousands are killed in a day... Young children are being tortured before their parents very eyes... Auschwitz is worse than hell."

Early the next morning the Polish student was taken out of the cell to be executed. Alfred was saved by Danish policemen when he was about to die from starvation. The policemen were prisoners in the Buchenwald camp where Alfred spent the last weeks of the war, and when they discovered that Alfred spoke Danish, they threw a coat and food to him over the barbed-wire fence, food which the Danish Red Cross had sent to the Danes.

The experiment of finding a new way of getting to Palestine was called off after yet another failed attempt. Three young Jews, Heinz, Ella and Ruth, tried to get to Turkey. They were captured by the Germans in Warnemünde. No one ever heard from them again. There were thirty members of the group left, six had been lost. At a meeting held outside the town of Sorø, they agreed to give up the experiment.

The choice was now between fleeing to Sweden or joining the Danish resistance movement. Hermann was among those who opted for the latter. He became a railway saboteur. The others fled to Sweden. After the war most of them went to Israel, where their Danish agricultural experience proved useful. They formed an association called "Dengang i Danmark" (In Those Days in Denmark).

This picture is from the Auschwitz death camp in Poland. The German soldier is inspecting Jews who have just arrived at the camp by freight car. The able-bodied ones were used for slave labor. The rest were sent to the gas chambers. Two-thirds of the Jews shown here were dead a few hours after the picture was taken.

DENOUNCED AND ARRESTED

Hermann was arrested at the end of 1943 in Odense, when he was riding one night with twenty pieces of plastic explosives on the back of his bicycle. He managed to get away. In his book *Konfrontationer* (Confrontations) (14) Hermann recounts:

> "Ausweiss bitte," the German said... I fumbled around in my pocket, "searching" for the pass I didn't have. It was now or never. I brought my hand out again and it landed as a clenched fist in the soldier's surprised face. Almost simultaneously I stepped down hard on the pedals, moving past the soldier and up hill.

The soldier shot at Hermann, but the latter disappeared around a corner and was saved – for now. Some months later he was denounced and subsequently arrested by the Gestapo. He was kicked and beaten and tortured by being hung by the wrists.

Hermann pretended to be a little backward and naive. When he admitted right away that he was Jewish, the Germans were convinced that he really was stupid.

He was sent to Sachsenhausen, together with 65 other Danes. Later he was separated from his Danish friends and sent to the Auschwitz death camp.

Shortly before the end of the war he was sent on a death march west, along with other prisoners.

The Germans were fleeing from the Russian army and forced many prisoners to accompany them on their flight. After two days they reached another prison camp, Gross Rosen, from which they were liberated by American soldiers.

Hermann returned to Denmark. Eventually he emigrated to Israel, where he worked as a farmer for many years, and later on as a teacher in Kibbutz Neot Mordechai in northern Galilee. In 1973 he returned to Denmark. He died in 1987.

In his book, Hermann Waldmann expresses his view of life after his experiences as a saboteur and concentration camp prisoner:

> Now I only know that the terrible time I experienced must never return, that Nazism and anti-Semitism must never again be allowed to thrive.

Hitler's absurd world. It had its roots in something we all know, something that is almost a natural condition, the fear of what is different, the hatred of what is different – agressions toward what is different. Hunting witches – hunting gypsies – hunting Jews.

A STORY OF SMUGGLING

David Israel returned to Denmark after his escape to Sweden. He had joined the resistance at a very early stage and had to flee to Sweden. After being expelled, he was arrested by the Danish police. First he spent a year in Vestre Prison and after that some months in Nyborg State Prison.

He was released in the middle of October 1943, after most Jews had escaped. He decided to go back to Sweden, but after some weeks he grew tired of the life of a refugee and returned illegally to Denmark.

Svend Erik Østerholm. After the occupation, he volunteered for the British army and served in India. Like David Israel, he was a soldier in the Danish Brigade during the refugee period in Sweden.

David Israe[l] [...] volunteer[ed] for the Israe[li] army in 194[...] and advanc[ed] to the rank [of] captain. H[e] was wound[ed] during a fig[ht] with Ar[ab] forces ar[...] now lives with his family in Israe[l].

His main purpose was to rescue the Jewish religious objects that had been abandoned in the synagogue on Krystal Street in Copenhagen. There were Torah scrolls with the Mosaic law, handwritten in Hebrew on parchment, prayer shawls which Jews wear over their shoulders in the synagogue and prayer books.

The Jews had left all of that behind when they fled. The priests of the Trinitatis Church adjoining Rundetårn (the Round Tower) had removed the ten Torahs that were placed in the Ark of the synagogue and had hidden them in the crypt beneath the floor of the Trinitatis Church, where they remained until the synagogue was reopened after the liberation. But the priests had overlooked a storage place where more than a hundred Torahs were kept.

David Israel knew this and broke into the synagogue in broad daylight together with a friend, Svend Erik Østerholm.

Østerholm recounts that the synagogue was a mess of bread crusts and Danish and German newspapers. The Germans had taken up quarters there, but apparently they had not vandalized the place.

Early one morning Østerholm and Israel broke open the main gate to the synagogue. The passers-by looked on in surprise. Some asked what they were doing, but were told that they had better go away. It was unwise to ask too many questions during the occupation. One never knew whether one would get into trouble with the Germans or their Danish helpers.

The two were aware that they were engaged in risky business. In the heart of Copenhagen there where swarms of German soldiers in green, and black-uniformed Gestapo men. One of the headquarters of the Danish Nazis was located some hundred meters away on the Kultorv Square.

Israel had prepared their retreat in advance. He had made arrangements with a skipper to be ready to sail them back to Sweden after they had finished emptying the synagogue of the objects. They had arranged with a company named Salicath, located on Tagensvej, to send some moving men with boxes to the synagogue. And David Israel had had a government official issue false freight papers, declaring that the boxes contained furniture belonging to a Danish engineer who had been given employment in Sweden.

After the Jews' flight to Sweden, the Torah scrolls which were kept in the Ark were saved by the priests of Trinitatis Church. The inscription above the Torahs is in Hebrew, the Biblical language which is spoken in Israel today. It is the Jews' declaration of faith: Hear O Israel, The Lord is our God, The Lord is One...

The Synagogue Is Emptied

Østerlund and Israel emptied the synagogue of everything. Finally, they unscrewed the two large, silver candlesticks from the altar. The moving men did the packing, and later in the day the engineer's "household items" were taken in large vans to Østerport Train Station. From here they were loaded onto a train which went to Sweden via the Helsingør ferry.

That same night, November 11, 1943, Østerholm and Israel wandered through Copenhagen harbor on their way to the sand-pump dredger that was to bring them to safety. Along the way they were stopped by a German guard, but when they showed him their false seaman's discharge books, he waved them on. On board they were hidden below, the hatch was bolted shut and they were in the dark with their feet in water.

Some hours later they were out of danger. A Swedish customs boat hailed them and took Østerholm on board. The sand-pump dredger let Israel off somewhere else, without the Swedes noticing it. He feared that he would once again be expelled by the Swedish police and rewarded for his efforts to save the holy scriptures by ending up for the second time in a Danish prison.

Both Østerholm and Israel stayed in Sweden for the remainder of the war. They enlisted with the Danish Brigade and returned to Denmark with it on May 5, Liberation Day.

David Israel signed up as a volunteer in the Israeli War of Liberation in 1948. He now lives in Israel. (15) Østerholm enlisted in the British army and served in India. He returned to Denmark in 1948.

THE INFORMER GIRL FROM GILLELEJE

The greatest misfortune that occurred during the evacuation of the Danish Jews took place in the town of Gilleleje, but there were many minor tragedies. In some cases Danish informers were responsible. In others, refugees were captured by German patrols, as in the case of Valdemar Koppel.

In his book *Flugten over Øresund* (The Flight Across The Sound), Torben Meyer tells about a group of 25 Jewish children, from six months to 15 years of age, who were deported the week prior to Christmas 1943. They had become separated from their parents, who had either been shot, or arrested and sent south. In some cases the parents had made it safely to Sweden, while the children for some reason or other had been abandoned. All these children had been placed in the German section of Vestre Prison. They were malnourished, ill and dirty when the Germans decided to deport them. (16)

There are stories such as the one about the maid who informed the German authorities about the Jews hiding out with the family she worked for. Her employers did not dare to fire her, for fear that she would complain to the Germans.

An informer was also responsible for the largest capture made by the Germans: 80 Jews were arrested in the attic of the Gilleleje Church.

The rescue transports from Gilleleje had so far gone well. Hundreds of Jews had been hidden in the fishing village, and on one occasion the departure had

It was in this church in Gilleleje, north of Copenhagen, that about 80 Jews were captured by the Germans while waiting for passage on a ship to Sweden. They had been betrayed by an informer and were transported to the Horserød camp. From there they were sent to Theresienstadt.

even taken place in broad daylight. A message had arrived that a schooner was ready to sail from the far end of the harbor. The Jews and their helpers rushed out onto the pier. Some old people were taken out in wheelbarrows; time was of the essence. The quay was swarming with people. The skipper cast off. When the schooner was 25 meters from the shore, German military vehicles rolled into the harbor area. They were too late. One hundred and eighty Jews had gotten away.

The following night 80 Jews were captured by the Gestapo in Gilleleje. The Gestapo had sealed off the harbor to prevent the refugees from getting away. The refugees' helpers feared that the Gestapo would search the town, house by house, so the Jews were directed outside the village to some farms in the area. The next morning they returned to Gilleleje. At 10 a.m. the Gestapo returned, and no one knew what to do, until one of the helpers suggested that some Jews take refuge in the attic of the church, while others would hide in the local parish hall.

The night passed. There were no toilet facilities, recounts a woman who was there, only some buckets in a corner, but no one could find them because of the darkness. It was forbidden to use matches, for fear that the Germans would discover where the Jews were hiding. The local people sent up food: soup and roast meat, but the refugees were not able to eat in the dark. At one point the priest of the church came and spoke some reassuring words to the Jews. Before leaving, he blessed them. This did not brighten their mood.

It was a cold October night in the attic. The hours passed, she recounts, and despair grew. There was a good deal of weeping that night. Late in the morning voices were heard outside the door to the attic. They were German. The hiding place had been revealed by a woman in town, it was said.

The Jews were hiding here in the attic of the Gilleleje Church the night they were captured. This is the only case where the Germans made a good catch.

Later it turned out that she was the girlfriend of a German soldier. Eight or ten Gestapo men entered, carrying revolvers and lanterns. *"Raus"* (Out), they shouted. One man broke down crying. The rest were paralyzed.

"We were taken to the parish hall, and a van took us to the Horserød camp. My young son and I were released after questioning, because my husband was not Jewish, but most of the others were deported."

The man who led the raid was Gestapo Officer Juhl from Helsingør. He later claimed that he had found the Jews in the attic by pure luck. He had come to search the church, and his suspicion was aroused when they refused to let him in. After that he and his men conducted a thorough search which brought them to the attic.

The Horserød Camp

The Germans gathered the Jews captured on Zealand in Horserød camp.

The writer Ralph Oppenhejm has described the scene in an autobiographical novel titled *Det skulle så være. Dagbog fra Theresienstadt* (It Came To Pass: A Theresienstadt Diary). (17)

On October 6, Oppenhejm made this entry in his diary:

> Today two sets of "catches" made in Gilleleje arrived... There are now 168 of us, my father says...

October 8:

> Yesterday there was a roll-call, and we were told that each of us would be allowed to write a card to an acquaintance, asking for clothing.

October 12:

> At this moment there was the sound of engines. The trucks were returning to collect us. On my way to the line-up, someone suddenly

> grabbed me by the arm. It was the prison guard. "Make sure to get into the last train car. You will receive help. Remember this," he whispered, and was gone. Then we left the Horserød camp... We were crowded into trucks with heavily armed soldiers.

But they did not receive help. The journey went via Warnemünde to Theresienstadt, the concentration camp in Czechoslovakia.

In his book, Oppenhejm tells of the capture of his family.

They had made contact with a helper who provided them with a rowboat that would hold eight persons. They set off from a landing stage in Rungsted. After a few hours, they realized that the boat was taking in water, and they had lost their sense of direction. A steamer was approaching. They were rowing like mad, but a few hundred yards away from the ship they were detected. A rope ladder was thrown down, and all eight of them climbed on board. The ship was on its way to Århus. At this point they were less than 25 minutes sailing time from a Swedish harbor.

The captain refused to bring the refugees to safety. It would cost him his job, he said. The mate tried to make him see reason, but did not succeed. Instead the captain summoned the pilot from Helsingør, who notified the Germans. A patrol boat came alongside the steamer. The family managed to swallow a mixture of brandy and morphine before the Germans arrived shouting, *"Heraus, sofort!"* but the poison did not work.

Oppenhejm and his family were taken to Helsingør where they were questioned. Ralph did not wake up until he was in the Horserød camp. The family survived both the poison and Theresienstadt and returned home after the war.

BIRGIT, FIVE YEARS OLD – A GERMAN PRISONER

Birgit Fischermann was seized by the Germans when she was five years old. She tells of her experiences (18):

It all began one day when my father did not come home. I sensed that my mother was very nervous. When a couple of days had gone by, my mother went to the Danish police and asked if they could find out what had happened to my father. They said that if my father had been taken into custody by the Danish police, he was safe. If he had been taken by the German police, he was lost.

My mother then went to the German headquarters in the Dagmarhus building (where prisoners were held) and inquired about father. They told her it was a good thing she had come, since my father would be arriving that very evening. My mother could come and pick him up then. She was to bring me along.

When we arrived at Dagmarhus in the evening, we were first asked to go down into a very dark room. This scared me so much that I started crying. Shortly after, we came up to the second floor. There I could feel that my mother became frightened. She said, "Oh no, this is the end." I realized that she said this because so many friends and acquaintances were sitting in the room into which we were taken. They had all been told to come to pick up their family members. Afterwards they would be released. We waited for a very long time in Dagmarhus, but my father did not appear.

We were driven by truck from Dagmarhus near the Town Hall Square to Langelinie Quay. If I had not noticed that the grown-ups were so scared, I probably would have enjoyed the ride. I found it exciting to ride in a truck. It was a pretty cold evening, so I was shivering. I did not have my warm cap to wear, I had forgotten it at home, so a much older girl gave me hers. It was blue with red polka-dots.

There were German soldiers all over, carrying rifles. They ordered us to line up and stand still, so we stood there for a very long time, facing the water. I finally started crying, for the whole thing was so strange. I was frightened and sensed that the grown-ups were too. Later on we were ordered to board some grey ships... We were directed into

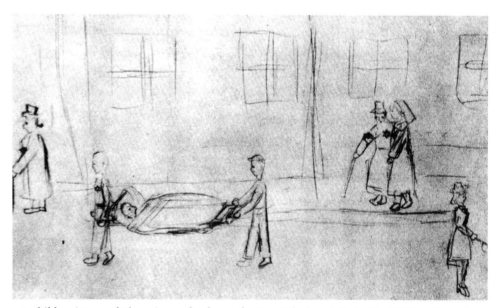

A child's picture of Theresienstadt, drawn by Eva Schulzová (July 20, 1931 – December 18, 1943). Fifteen thousand children were sent from Theresienstadt to death camps in Poland. Eva was gassed in Auschwitz.

the very bottom of the ship. A little later my father came. He had been in Vestre Prison, and his face looked strange, because he had not shaved or washed for several days. I had never seen him looking like that before.

Father had tried to get a fisherman to sail us to Sweden, but a neighbor had told the Gestapo, who showed up and brought everyone in the apartment in for questioning.

A little later my grandparents came on board the ship; they had brought their blankets for sleeping. My aunt and uncle were there, too.

When we came ashore, we were told that we were in Germany. We had to climb down an iron ladder and my mother was very frightened, because she was pregnant.

I do not know how long we rode in the cattle cars. When the train finally stopped and we came out of the cars, we were counted. All valuables were to be handed over, and we were given a star on which it said "Jude." I was given one, too. There were many children. In the camp where I was, there were 60,000 people, but there was only room for half that many.

A girl with whom I played got lice. She had all of her hair cut off. I felt sorry for her, so I gave her my knitted cap. One day she was gone, and nobody knew what had happened to her.

A Danish delegation came to the camp in the spring of 1944. They were to be shown the conditions under which the Danish prisoners were living. The whole camp was tidied up. All the old and sick people were not allowed anywhere near the visitors. A kind of playroom was arranged very nicely, but we were only permitted to use it while the delegation was there.

In the spring of 1945, just before the war ended, many children were sent to the gas chambers. All in all, 1.5 million children from the camps were gassed.

One day my father came up to me. He wanted to show me some white busses with a red cross on them. He told me that these busses would take us back to Denmark. The next day we were able to go home on the busses.

When we arrived in Denmark, we were not allowed to stay there. We had to continue to Sweden right away. When we got there, my brother and I had chicken pox, and because it itched a lot, we had slices of cucumber placed on our skin. Shortly after, I took the cucumber slices off and ate them. It had been so long since I had tasted cucumber.

When we had been in Sweden for a month, my father went to Denmark to look for work and find an apartment. When he had succeeded in doing so, he came to pick us up. And then we returned home.

On Board the "Wartheland"

The brothers Johan and Olaf Grün were arrested by German soldiers while they were on their way from Nivå Brickworks to a boat that was to bring them to Sweden. Johan recalls:

> We were asked whether we were Jewish, and we had to answer in the affirmative, of course. Afterwards we were taken to an assembly point in Vedbæk. Here we had to wait for two or three hours until we were taken to Langelinie Quay in German military trucks.
>
> A large German freighter, the "Wartheland," was anchored there, waiting for its cargo – the first transport of Danish Jews to Theresienstadt. On the pier we had to wait yet another couple of hours before being hustled on board. To embark, we had to walk up a very narrow plank to the uppermost deck, and from there we had to descend a great number of stairs leading all the way down into the bottom of the ship, into the hold which had been restructured to contain a cargo of prisoners.
>
> We were met by the distressing sight of our friends and relatives lying there. I have a clear memory of our Rabbi, Dr. Max Friediger, coming forward to greet us, saying: "So you are here too."

It was terrible to see the old people from the Krystalgade nursing home in Copenhagen lying there, wailing and crying. An elderly lady from the nursing home, unable to walk up the stairs, had been placed on a mattress and was lifted on board by a crane. She was in great pain, as the mattress had doubled up during the rough transfer from the pier.

If we needed to go to the toilet, we had to climb up a very steep stairway to a foul room guarded by German soldiers who informed us that we were about to sail off to Germany. There was no toilet paper whatsoever in this "toilet."

Early the next morning we arrived in Swinemünde where we all had to descend the stairs again. On the pier we had to climb into a row of cattle cars; this was very difficult, and the young had to help the old. Each car had to hold 55 or 60 people, nearly every centimeter had to be used. A space was also needed for a bucket with a little water for drinking, and a bucket also had to serve as a toilet for 56 desperate people for three or four days! On our way through Germany we were aired a few times in the course of a day, however, so the toilet bucket was not used that much. In our car it was mostly used by the children.

A little girl, a couple of years old, who had been terribly frightened by the whole sinister situation, wanted to sit only next to me for the duration of the transport. She did not want to have anything to do with her parents.

On the other side of me lay an elderly German Jewish emigrant, and on the first morning I sensed that he had grown strangely stiff during the night. He had died from some pills he had swallowed, suspecting what might happen to us all.

Before the war, cattle cars were made with a brake compartment at one end of the car, quite high up, with a stairway leading up to a small observation tower where the brake wheels used for shunting the freight cars were kept. The body of the dead man was placed there upright, and it swayed back and forth, making an eerie sound for the next four days of the journey.

The Jews were transported to extermination like cattle. The trip from Holland and France to Poland where the death camps were located could take up to two weeks. There was no food or drink during the journey, and many victims died of hunger.

From Denmark, we arrived in Theresienstadt, one of the concentration camps in Europe that had the best conditions.

When we arrived in Theresienstadt, we soon became familiar with hunger and misery. We all lost weight. I lost 36 kilos. We were given 50 grams of "margarine," half a kilo of bread and 50 grams of sugar every fourth day, and had to work very hard. It was not long before our rations were consumed. We then lived off the grey soup that was dished out from the kitchen every day.

When we arrived, there were about 85,000 prisoners from Holland, France, Germany, Czechoslovakia, Rumania, Austria and Hungary living there – and then came the Danes. It was a transit camp with a very high turnover.

New prisoners arrived continually, and transports often left from there for Auschwitz, where the journey ended. The only exit from these death camps was through the chimneys of the gas chambers.

When transports were due to leave, it was hard to be a human being. For when the Germans ordered a transport ready in the course of two or three days, the Jewish "Elder Council" was to see to it that the 5,000 to 6,000 prisoners were selected. Families were separated; children were separated from their parents and married couples were separated, never to see each other again. The most appalling scenes took place

Theresienstadt was a barracks-town in Czechoslovakia that was taken over by the Germans and converted to a concentration camp. The Danish Jews were among the rare permanent residents of the camp during the war. For most others, Theresienstadt was a transit station on the way to the death camps.

when prisoners came into the administration office to try to preserve what was left of their family. The number of prisoners demanded by the Germans had to be rounded up by any means, even if it meant using force.

Other prisoners were told to chase their own people into the cattle cars, 50-60 prisoners in each, at the local railway station, the most sinister of its kind. SS-soldiers were also ordered to help get the wretched prisoners into the cars which were then locked – and theirs was not gentle help. Imagine what it was like to send 6,000 orphaned children off on their last journey. It cannot be described.

Some of the transports arriving in Theresienstadt were also grim. I remember when a transport came from Holland with about 2,000 prisoners who had been locked up in cattle cars for about ten days with hardly anything to eat or drink. They had gone completely mad, and never became human again. Some of them stayed in the town, others were sent to the gas chambers. It may have been the best thing for them.

For a whole day and a whole night in November 1943, all the prisoners in the camp, about 80,000, were taken out into a field – escorted by German soldiers – in order to be counted. As we were not allowed anything to eat or drink, many collapsed from exhaustion. Many of us were damaged for life. Twelve Danes died shortly after these hardships.

One day something happened! There were rumors that a Danish delegation from the Red Cross and the Foreign Ministry was coming. On June 23, 1944, a delegation arrived, which consisted of Frantz Hvass, head of a branch of the Foreign Ministry, and Dr. Eigil Juel Henningen from the Red Cross. They spent seven or eight hours with us to see how we lived.

We were only allowed to speak in German, so that the Germans who accompanied them could check what was said. One of the Danes succeeded in whispering to me, "We bring you personal greetings from King Christian X, and prayers will be said for you in all the churches of the country this coming Sunday." I was so touched by this that tears ran down my cheeks. When the Germans asked me what was the matter, I answered that it was a reaction to meeting people from my native country.

One day, when 19 1/2 months had gone by, a couple of Danes claimed that they had seen a Red Cross car on the outskirts of Theresienstadt, and that now we would be taken home. And on April 14, 1945, all Danes were told to gather in a barrack and be ready to be picked up there!

Outside the barrack, Red Cross busses – with red crosses clearly painted on their sides and roofs – were waiting for us.

On April 15, we drove out of the town while an orchestra formed by prisoners played a farewell for us.

On April 13, 1945, the Danish prisoners in the Theresienstadt concentration camp were told that they were going home. On the 14th, they started their trip in the white busses that had come from Denmark to bring the prisoners home.

Now we are done for, said the other prisoners who had to stay behind. There were about 60,000 of them.

The journey to Sweden went through a devastated Germany. We drove north through the war zone toward the Danish border, with Russians on one side of us and Englishmen and Americans on the other. Several times we had to get out when bombs were dropped close to our 23 busses with their 423 surviving Danish prisoners.

All over, dead horses and people were lying in the roads. There was chaos everywhere. But we did finally reach the Danish border.

When we drove into Denmark, we wept with joy to see our native land again, but we also thought of our friends who had died away from it. Danish women in Red Cross uniforms threw chocolate, cigarettes and flowers to us.

On the first day we came to the town of Odense, where we were put up at the Y.M.C.A. and served steak and potatoes. But after all those months, our stomachs had become unused to all the things we had been looking forward to eating. On the ferry going across The Great Belt, the toilets were in constant use, but this time, fortunately, there was no shortage of toilet paper.

When we arrived in Copenhagen, we were taken to the Free Port, where we were to board a ferry to Malmø in Sweden. In the harbor, many people stood waving to us, shouting "Welcome home."

We then arrived in Malmø, where we were deloused and split up into two camps. My brother Olaf and I came to Tyløsand near Halmstad, to an internment camp. There we were to stay until the end of the war.

On the 4th of May, we heard the freedom-message from London. In the evening we all gathered and sent a congratulatory telegram to King Christian X. The following day we received the King's thank-you telegram. About a month later we returned to our homes in Copenhagen. Little by little we could begin our everyday lives again, but we all carried permanent scars from our stay abroad. (19)

The Night on Langelinie Quay

There is only one Danish description of what happened on Langelinie Quay on the night of October 1-2. It is written by the physician Hans Keiser-Nielsen, known under his cover name "Doc." That night a large German battleship was anchored at the Langelinie Quay. "Doc" had decided that he would sabotage it from the water with a magnetic bomb. While engaged in this operation, he became a witness to the deportation of the Jews captured by the Germans in the course of the night.

Keiser-Nielsen writes:

> I had been "fishing" just outside the roped-off area on Langelinie Quay, as close to the battleship as possible, to make sure that the current actually went from here and straight along the side of the battleship. After numerous experiments, I had produced a large – very large – underwater bomb with long "arms" sticking out of it and magnets attached to their ends. The whole thing was balanced on air cushions, so that the bomb was submerged about a meter under the surface of the water with only a little black float awash. Fastened onto this were two very long, thin lines with which to guide the bomb as it drifted downstream.
>
> It had been made and tested in the Danish Students' boat house and the basin outside it, that is to say, quietly and unobserved. It seemed to work perfectly.
>
> And then one night, between the first and second of October, I was lying on the deck of the "Tjalfe" (the ship belonging to the amateur sailing club). I had the two lines coming out of two scuppers and the bomb – completely invisible – was on its course toward the battleship. But this was where the complication that never fails to arise in any act of sabotage occurred. The current now slipped into a little, still channel just in front of the battleship. This I had not been able to see when I was fishing! So everything had to be hauled in again, and I had to fetch the bomb out of the water; but by now I felt so angry and disappointed

that I – admittedly – cast everything to the winds, including good sense...

I tied one of the lines around my waist and pulled myself along the pier towards the enemy. The guards on deck, the occasional, sweeping search light, nothing could stop me, I thought. But blessed providence (as I am indeed prepared to think) put an end to this madness, by very imaginative means: phosphorescence! I discovered that I shone brightly with sparkling phosphorescence at the slightest movement.

So, as a result, my life was saved this time around. I crawled into hiding on deck, changed to some dry clothes I had brought along and wiped the black make-up off my face and hands. And so I was ready, just at that moment, to witness the tragedy that unrolled before me: Here in the early dawn a truck came driving out along the uppermost pier of the Langelinie Quay, moving toward a large ship at the far end of it. And just barely visible out there was a gangplank leading from the pier to the ship. Along this, one small figure after another, hundreds of them, came walking, many of them very slowly, bent over, a few with baby carriages, and disappeared into the ship.

Later in the morning when there was no curfew, some of them could be seen returning by the long gangplank, very slowly. They had apparently been "acquitted," were not allowed to join their relatives... I mingled with some small groups of these "rejected" Jews in the yachting harbor area. But I could not stay... had to quickly go home. It was an evil night. (20)

SALOMON, HELLE AND FRIDA

Salomon Katz was one of the Danish Jews who, till the last, refused to believe that it could happen here. He ended up in Theresienstadt.

He has written a diary in which he describes his arrest (21):

> From mid-September, 1943, there were rumors that several ships were anchored along the Langelinie Quay, and that they were intended for the Jews. But there were so many rumors going about at the time, so I did not believe them... I kept saying that there would be no persecution of the Jews, but it happened even so. On the second of October, Helle, Frida and I were awakened at 1:30 in the morning by a ringing at the door. I had already heard heavy steps on the stairs and knew instantly that it was the Germans coming to take us away.
>
> There were four German gendarmes and a Danish-speaking man, who asked me if I was the owner of the apartment, and when I answered yes, he told us to get dressed and come along. The Germans, I must say, were not so bad. The Dane, on the other hand, was a real bully. He had allowed us twenty minutes to get dressed, and when the twenty minutes were up, he began to hurry us up, did not want to waste his time waiting for us. I happened to look over at the German standing by

the door and noticed that he was looking down on the floor, his head lowered, as if ashamed of the whole situation.

When we came down into the street, we began to walk toward Strand Boulevard. Along the way I asked the man whether he thought that things would improve in Denmark now that the Jews were being seized.

"You bet it will, kike," he said. "You are the ones responsible for the sabotage"...

"You will learn," I said. "Shut up," he answered.

Going along Kalkbrænderi Street, we had reached Randers Street where a covered truck was parked in the middle of the road.

This truck drove around and collected Jews who had been seized. It was joined by other trucks carrying Jews. It was five o'clock in the morning, and the first trams were beginning to run. The trucks drove toward Langelinie Quay where three steamers were moored. The Jews were chased on board. Their baggage was searched and tobacco and shaving equipment, knives and forks were confiscated. Then they were made to go down into the hold. Here Salomon Katz found his father, mother and sister.

The ship sailed to Swinemünde.

At 10 o'clock in the evening on October 5, after four days of transportation, they arrived at the Theresienstadt concentration camp. Here they were to spend 18 months in captivity, in constant fear of being sent east to the death camps and the gas chambers.

"Countrymen, Don't Lose Your Courage"

There were also 150 Danish communists on board the "Wartheland" transporting the Jews to Germany. They had been arrested by the Danish police on June 22, 1941, and taken to the Horserød camp. From here they were transported to Langelinie Quay by the Germans and placed below the foredeck of the ship. The Jews were placed astern.

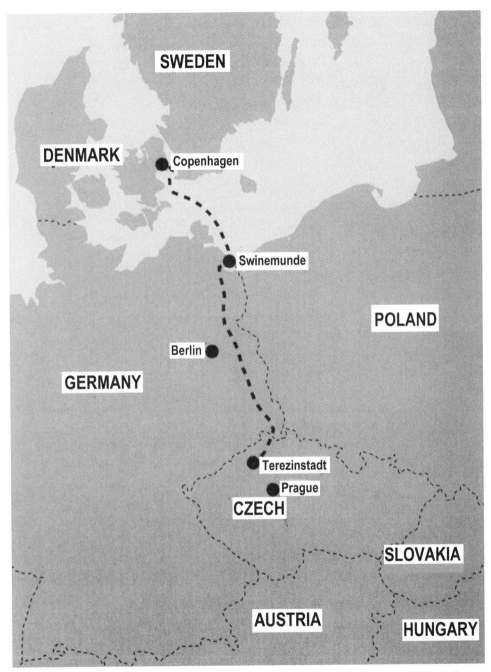

The route to Theresienstadt. The transport left at 10:24 a.m on October 2, 1943, from Langelinie to Swinemünde in Germany and continued via cattle car to Theresienstadt. The Danish prisoners arrived at the concentration camp on October 5 at about 10 p.m.

The Danes were the only prisoners in Theresienstadt allowed to receive food parcels. These were distributed via the Danish Red Cross. The Germans allowed friends and acquaintances to send packages. Often, the sender, in this case Ruth Bredsdorff, did not know the recipient, Nachmann Levin. The parcels were financed both by private contribution and by the Ministry of Social Affairs.

Upon arrival in Swinemünde, the prisoners were hustled onto the pier. The Jews and the communists were separated, as they were not going to the same concentration camp. The Germans ordered an inspection, and the prisoners were lined up in rows. A dead silence reigned. Only the Germans were shouting. Then something happened which remains fixed in the memory of many Danish Jews.

One of the communists, Frode Toft, stepped out in front of his friends, turned toward the Jews who were on their way to an unknown fate and in a clear voice shouted, "Countrymen, hold your heads up high."

Marcus Choleva, who was then a boy, remembers the episode. And today, 50 years later, Johan Grün says, "I shall never forget that. It kept us from losing our courage completely."

Almost all Danish Jews survived the captivity in Theresienstadt, thanks, in part, to the attempts made by the Danish authorities to protect them. They were given preferential treatment by the Germans, and the Danish Red Cross sent packages with food and medicine. The Germans stole much of it along the way, but what remained was enough to keep the Danish Jews alive. Friends in Denmark sent clothing into which they had sewn vitamin pills.

It is perhaps hard to imagine, but the personal greeting from King Christian X, which Johan Grün mentions in his report from Theresienstadt, really helped bolster the morale of the Danish Jews. Their countrymen had not forgotten them.

No Danish Jews were deported from Theresienstadt to the extermination camps in Poland. Out of the 474 who were captured, only about 10% died – of old age or disease. Almost 99% of the Danish Jews survived the war and the Nazi persecutions. Half of Norway's 1,800 Jews perished. In Poland there were 3.3 million Jews before the war. Only 300,000 survived. We got off lightly.

Martin Nielsen witnessed the arrival of the Danish Jews in Swinemünde, Germany. He was one of the 150 communists placed in the bow of the "Wartheland." They were the first to be ordered off the ship and lined up on the pier. Then it was the Jews' turn. Nielsen and his comrades had been in isolation in the Horserød camp; they knew nothing of the persecution of the Jews in Denmark.

The following is his description, written on his return home, after having survived 20 months in German concentration camps.

With Screams and Shouts and Kicking

We felt a shock when suddenly, from below the stern, a great number of Danish Jews emerged. We had been exposed to humiliation and scorn during our passage from Copenhagen, but it was nothing in comparison to what we were now about to witness.

We estimated the number of Danish Jews to be around 200. They were of all ages, from infants in their mother's arms to old, trembling women and old men supporting themselves on two canes. They seemed to represent all walks of life, from young intellectual-looking men to long-bearded Jews wearing peasant coats and skullcaps, such as you would see before the war in the Borgergade and Adelgade quarters.

Even before we had recovered from our surprise at this disturbing sight, the Gestapo men, uttering the most unbelievable curses and oaths, began to chase the wretched, sorely-tried people down the very steep gangplank. One of the first to walk down the gangplank was a very young woman carrying an infant, hardly more than six months old. The child was crying, and the mother was gently calming it down. She seemed not to hear the lewd mockery from the master race, but merely clasped her precious burden to her breast. The youngest Jews were the first to descend. On the pier they calmly – much too calmly, I was thinking – lined up in rows, with their backs turned to the gangplank. It was as if the screaming and shouting from the Gestapo men did not reach their ears at all. After the young ones had descended, a scene unfolded which we shall never forget. Later on, in the hell of Stutthof, on our long death march down the icy roads of the Polish Corridor and Pomerania, we experienced, and some of us survived, far more cruel things than what we saw that October morning in Swinemünde, and yet these are the events that have so burned themselves into our memories that we shall never ever be able to forget them.

Why?

Ask any Danes who survived Swinemünde and Stutthof, and they will all give you the same answer:

Because on that morning we were still human beings who thought and felt like human beings, whose brains and nerves were still responding in a human way. Later on, our feelings and our nerves had been coarsened to such an extent that far crueller incidents did not make a comparable impression on us. Gradually we became immune to bestialities, cruelty and horror.

So what was it that made such an indelible impression on us? It was the fact that when all the young and strong Jews had reached the pier, the ones who were left on deck were all the sick ones, all the old, bent-over and trembling ones, all the unbelievably exhausted and poor-looking Jews who, according to the gospel of the master race, were responsible not only for the war but for each and every evil in this sinful world.

Young, energetic, well-fed, clean-shaven and well-groomed Gestapo officers danced a veritable war dance on the deck around these "truly guilty" of the war. They chased these wretched souls down the steep gangplank with kicks, shoves and blows. These people, frightened out of their wits, tried as best they could to totter down the gangway, but literally could not. They fell, they clutched the ropes along the gangway, they tried to feel their way forward with their feet and canes. Many of them obviously had trouble seeing. Most likely the master race had stolen, "organized," their glasses. Gold-rimmed glasses, at any rate, always became the spoils of the master race.

A couple of half-grown boys around 16 or 17 were running up and down the gangway trying as best they could to help and support their wretched relatives. After a while, the Gestapo men with their shouting, shoving and kicking had, of course, made the old people completely confused. They were at their wit's end, simply huddling together like animals in a storm. Then suddenly a couple of well-nourished Gestapo officers from the deck threw themselves onto the cluster of people on the gangway, pushing, shoving and kicking the old people down, making them tumble and roll down the plank onto the pier.

The master race enjoyed themselves immensely.

Still left on deck was just one old – extremely old – wrinkled and shivering woman. She was overwhelmed by fear and terror. As if in a seizure, she clung to the ropes along the gangway, and shrill, hysterical screams came from her pained throat. In one great leap the Gestapo chief himself was standing on the plank below the old woman. In utter rage he tore out his revolver and for a brief moment aimed it at the old woman's head.

Now he is going to shoot her, I thought.

But no. Instead he turns the revolver the other way around, holds the barrel in his right hand and with short, rapid blows brings it down on the old woman's skinny hands, still desperately clinging to the ropes. A wild, piercing scream is heard. The old woman lets go of her grip, she topples over, and with the aid of a well-directed kick by the Gestapo chief's boot, she rolls down the gangway and onto the ground.

Has that man never had a mother himself, I am thinking, closing my eyes. I cannot take any more. When I open my eyes again, I see the two half-grown boys dragging yet another old woman down the gangway. They do not have enough strength left to carry her, so the old woman's behind keeps bumping against the ribs of the gangway.

This is how the unloading of the "truly guilty" of the war, the Danish Jews, ended on that October morning in Swinemünde. (22)

AN ESCAPE ROUTE IS SET UP

Ole Helweg is an architect. He has written a book in which he describes the setting-up of one of the most important escape routes during the occupation: Dansk-Svensk Flygtningetjeneste (The Danish-Swedish Refugee Service).

From October 1943 until the end of the war, the Refugee Service made 367 trips back and forth between Sweden and Denmark carrying refugees, as well as 500 trips carrying mail, secret-intelligence material and weapons. A total of 1,880 adults and children were brought to safety in Sweden. Only two were captured by the Germans due to carelessness. One Danish refugee even had his bicycle sent illegally from Denmark.

On December 7, 1943, the Refugee Service's passenger list shows that 27 people and a six-year-old male wire-haired terrier were transported illegally across The Sound. (25)

Helweg is Danish but was living in Sweden during the war. He worked as an architect in Stockholm. The day the Swedish newspapers announced that "Danish citizens of Jewish descent are being arrested and taken to Germany," he decided to go into action.

"We knew nothing of what had happened in Copenhagen," he writes. "Had all of the 6,000 Danish Jews already been seized? Should I go to Copenhagen

My escape route: On Wednesday, September 29, 1943, by taxi from Kristiania Street in Copenhagen to friends in Lyngby. On Thursday, the 30th, by private car from the suburb of Lyngby to the village of Sletten, where we found shelter with a fisherman and his family who had been our hosts during summer vacations. Thursday night, a failed attempt to escape from a villa near the coast outside of Sletten. Friday, October 1, from Sletten by physician's car to Ålsgårde, north of Helsingør (Elsinore), where we were hidden by acquaintances. The same night, around 10 p.m., German gendarmes begin to arrest Jews in Copenhagen. All telephones are disconnected. At dawn, Saturday, October 2, we board a rowboat at Ålsgårde Beach and are rowed out to a fishing boat. The anchor is weighed, and 37 minutes later we are safe in Swedish territorial waters.

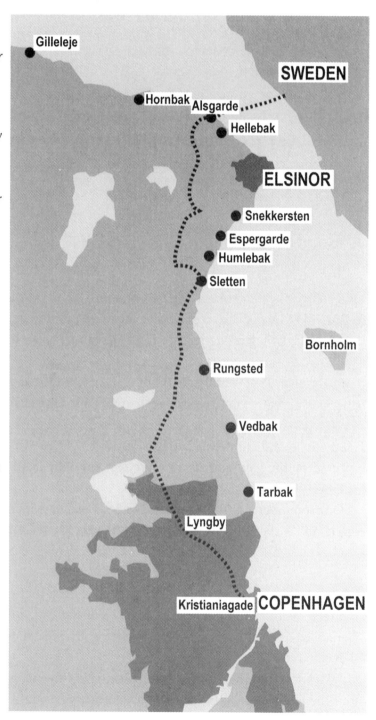

now and look for contacts? They must come to Sweden, of course. But that means getting hold of boats to take them across..."

He asked for a meeting with the Swedish Foreign Minister, Christian Günther, who was his wife's uncle. Afterwards he went to see Ebbe Munck, who was the representative of the Danish resistance in Sweden.

Through Munck and through Jewish circles in Sweden, Helweg got enough money together to buy a speedboat in Gøteborg. The boat was brought to Malmø, close to the Danish Coast.

Günther helped secure support for the operation from the Swedish authorities. In January 1943, the Soviet Union defeated the German army at Stalingrad. In September the Italians had surrendered, but the Allies had not won the war yet. The Swedes still had respect for the German weapons and, at least officially, adhered to their policy of neutrality.

The speedboat was the start of the Danish-Swedish Refugee Service which, until the end of the war, sailed back and forth, bringing hundreds of refugees and people from the resistance movement, as well as mail and weapons, across The Sound.

As in so many other situations, it was one man's initiative and determination that set things moving.

Munck left the management of the route to another refugee, an editor at the Danish newspaper *Ekstra Bladet*, Leif B. Hendil. Together they secretly traveled to Denmark to organize the Danish side of the operation. (23)

"Julius" – A Fishing Boat from Bornholm

In the meantime the Service had acquired another vessel, "Julius," a fishing boat from the island of Bornholm in the Baltic Sea. The boat was manned by three young Jews, refugees from Germany, who had been trained as fishermen on Bornholm. They spoke the Bornholm dialect, which to German ears could sound like Swedish.

This was what saved one of them, Erik Marx, when the "Julius" was seized one day by the Germans. Marx, as well as his Danish mates, among whom was Helweg, all had Swedish seamen's papers.

Perhaps the Germans were convinced, perhaps not. All three of them were released after being detained and questioned for a while in Vestre Prison. They were given German permission to sail the "Julius" back to Sweden. Two Gestapo officers escorted them to the boat and waved goodbye to them.

The "Julius" could hold 80 people if they were packed tightly together below. It picked up refugees in three places in southern Zealand. One place was on the coast off the beech forest belonging to Gjorslev Estate. The owner of the estate was Edward Tesdorpf. He placed his hunting lodge, which was only a few hundred meters from the beach, at their disposal.

Often the procedure was that the refugees were transported from, for instance, Bispebjerg Hospital to Vanløse Station, where they bought a return-trip ticket to the town of Køge. Here they were picked up by a taxicab driver and taken to the hunting lodge.

It is difficult to get a complete picture of the circumstances surrounding the escape of the Jews. Those involved experienced the various situations from their own personal angle. Only a few had a full view of it all.

The resistance movement was a silent organization. Its members were not to know any more than was strictly necessary to carry out their jobs. The less you knew about your friends and matters that did not concern you personally, the better. That set a limit to what you would be able to tell the Germans in case you were caught and exposed to what they called "severe questioning," that is to say, torture.

BEING A REFUGEE IN KØGE

A Helper's Account

Karen-Lykke Poulsen was one of the helpers involved in the two shipments from Gjorslev Beach.

She writes:

> I was living at the South Harbor with a fellow called Ole Haslund. The author Tove Dit-levsen was our neighbor. She has described the environment in her novel *Gift*.
>
> The night after the arrest of the Jews, one of my rather odd friends from the inner city came to me with a message that I was to help get people to Sweden. I was to show up the next afternoon on the main square in Køge. There I was to see what I could do.

So I showed up on the square. Some fellow I knew from the university took hold of me and told me to clear the square of refugees and send them to the town of Strøby. Afterwards I was to empty the woods south of Køge.

At that time the order sounded quite understandable and reasonable, but looking at it in retrospect, it seems completely crazy that I did not tell him that he must be out of his mind. Before he rushed on, he shouted, "The password is 'Oil on the Mountain'..." I did not ask what the devil I was to use that for.

On the square there were at least 100 people in groups of four to eight persons, swarthy and winter-clad, carrying suitcases. There were also some taxis.

I threw myself into the crowd of people and said, "Oil on the Mountain," right and left. I stuffed people into taxis and told them to go to the town of Strøby Egede.

Some of the most frightened ones had hidden themselves in woods and shrubbery along the roadside south of Køge, but we managed to get them all transported to Strøby Egede. It was late in the evening and getting dark when I arrived. This was the largest of all the transports...

The idea was that after dark the boat would anchor 50 meters from the coast. Then we were to row the refugees out to the boat.

When I got out to the coast, they had begun to row the people out. Three or four rowboats shuttled back and forth between a small pier and the boat.

There were not many helpers. Most of them were busy at the oars. As far as I could tell, I was the only girl helping.

The actor Hans-Henrik Krause participated as a helper under his own name. This surprised me. After a while I was told to gather people into groups and lead them from the clearing down onto the beach.

I still remember that I was filled with terror at the responsibility of having to pick out the people who were to go first. I am still so impressed with the discipline with which these hundreds of refugees willingly let themselves be ordered about in the pitch-black darkness by a young girl. They peacefully left their luggage behind and considerately yielded their place to others who they deemed had to go first.

As long as everything went well, there were no cracks in the bourgeois surface. Here and there I saw a face I knew from the lunch room at the university. I think this was the shipment that included the writer Otto Gelsted.

At any rate we managed to bring all of them out to the boat, and shortly before midnight it set out on its course eastward. We drove into Køge and made it to a bar at midnight, just before closing time. There we had a glass of cheap fruit-wine and looked each other over before riding back to Copenhagen in the taxis. It was at this bar that we suddenly experienced an attack of laughing cramps. I remember lying across the table howling with laughter, because we suddenly noticed one of these usual bar paintings on the wall. It was a picture of a sailing vessel and underneath it, in old-fashioned script, it said, "From here we ship whatever we want." It doesn't seem very funny now, but at the time, after 8 to 10 hours of extreme stress, it was just the funniest thing in the world. (26)

A Refugee's Account

The refugees experienced the situation from another angle. Here is the same operation, described by Ulf Ekman, who fled with his Jewish wife Ruth:

> The trip to Køge was completely uneventful. All I remember is that at a certain point the chauffeur leaned back in his seat and told us that he was surprised we had not been stopped by a German patrol. That had happened to him a few days ago. "These days," he said, "the Germans take a great interest in who is leaving town."
>
> This statement made us a bit uneasy, of course, but we reached our destination safely and went out onto the platform of the train station. Here a crowd of people had gathered, among whom I recognized the poet Otto Gelsted, a declared communist and a very impractical person,

whom the party, for his own sake as well as theirs, wanted to send away.

I also saw the physician and nutritionist, later-to-be professor, Poul Astrup, with whom I was slightly acquainted from the Students' Association of which he was vice chairman, I think. Astrup greeted me and asked if I had brought any money along. When I answered in the affirmative, he asked me without further ado to give it to him, which I did. It should be noted that a thousand kroner at that time probably would correspond to twenty thosand kroner ($ 3,000) at today's value.

Then for a good while nothing happened, and we began to get a bit nervous. What had we let ourselves in for? But suddenly we were given the signal to leave. An odd procession moved into the streets of Køge, carrying luggage in their hands, all dressed in heavy coats and furs even though it was a warm, sunny day and dead calm. A passer-by might not notice, but some of the women were wearing a conspicuous amount of jewelry. One of them was wearing so many rings on her fingers that she could barely bend them. In short, we could not avoid calling attention to ourselves. I was thinking, of course, that if even one Nazi were to notice us, he could easily notify the Germans, with dire consequences for all of us. But no one accosted us or did anything. We arrived safely at a place on the outskirts of town, where we climbed on a number of trucks. Tarpaulins were placed over the body of the truck, making it impossible for us to look out, and for anyone to see us. Then we drove for what seemed to me quite a long time until we reached our destination, a god-forsaken place on the coast which I was later told is called Strøby.

There was nothing to see other than a landing and a ship – a ketch, I think – all in all a very welcome sight. We were brought on board immediately.

Among those who helped the old ladies climb over the railing was a well-known actor, Hans-Henrik Krause, I believe, who was dressed in a light cotton coat with a belt – like the one Humphrey Bogart used to wear when he played a tough guy in the movies. This is the kind of totally irrelevant detail that for some reason leaves a particularly strong impression in your memory.

When we arrived, there were already quite a few people on board. Apparently they had reached Strøby by a different route. And, as far as I remember, more came later. All in all, there must have been a couple of hundred of us. We were all sent into the hold.

When we were all gathered, the skipper appeared, and to my great surprise he introduced himself by name, which I found reckless. His name was Sikker Hansen, and he was the brother of the very popular artist of that name. He was from the town of Dragør and normally made his living fishing up boulders from the sea floor, a profession which causes amusement in mountainous Sweden and Norway. There was something about his person that inspired confidence. It probably had to do with the fact that he was a strong-looking man, jovial by nature, with the gift of the gab and a forceful baritone voice. He told us that we could be reasonably hopeful. There were no Germans nearby, neither on land nor at sea. We were likely to have a good trip.

With these words, which were like manna to us, we set off and began to chug across The Sound. By now it had grown dark around us, and we were allowed to go up on deck. I availed myself of the opportunity to take a look around, together with Ruth, and to our great surprise and joy we discovered that all of her family – father, mother, grandmother and brother – were among the passengers. Her father did not know that the others were on board. The same was true of her brother. But now the family was united again for a short while.

During our crossing, just as we began to think that now we were almost safe, fate would have it that one of the ship's engines stalled. For a quarter of an hour we were helplessly adrift at sea. But fortunately the skipper got it started again, and we were able to resume our nocturnal journey, which then was suddenly interrupted by a bright searchlight hitting the ship. Behind the light we caught a glimpse of a patrolboat with a man standing at the bow. He had a megaphone in his hand and spoke the memorable words:

Ni skall alla vara hjärtlig välkomna i Sverige! (You are all most heartily welcome to Sweden!)

Ever since then, I have considered Swedish the loveliest language in the world. (27)

The Germans Are Coming

The next time it did not go as smoothly, Karen-Lykke Poulsen recounts:

It had been decided that yet another transport was to leave from Strøby Egede. This time we were scraping the bottom of the barrel. Now it was all the poor ones, the sick ones, those without contacts, who had to go. I recall this trip as a chaotic jumble of comical and awful incidents.

For two days we rushed around Copenhagen to call on all the people whose addresses we had obtained. Some were frightened, many were relieved. There were many taxis involved in the affair, as well as several ambulances from Bispebjerg Hospital. Gradually a great many helpers had become involved, and that was catastrophic. There were those from the previous transport, and there was Professor Richard Ege and his people, as well as a slew of idiots in breeches and jackboots from the University Rifles Club. From the beginning, a state of confrontation existed between them and the rest of us.

When we arrived, the small field in front of the gamekeeper's cottage was filled with cars, taxis and ambulances. I told them that they were out of their minds, of course, but the leader of the Rifles said that they had put up a flag, so that if the Germans came, they would tell them that they were celebrating a wedding anniversary at the house.

I was not very wise, and I have no idea what gave me the courage, but I scolded them, swearing like a fishmonger, and ordered them to hide all those cars.

My loud-mouthed behavior must have made Professor Ege trust me, for he asked me to see to it that the parked cars were scattered. He also gave me a shoebox full of money. I have never in my life had that much money in my hands. I had had to pawn my fountain pen for ten kroner at a pawnbroker's as far away as Enghave Square, in order to have enough money for the train ticket to Køge. At that time that fountain pen was the most valuable thing I owned. Cash on the line for the sale of my virtue. It had been received on the occasion of an engagement, with rings and everything, which had broken up the year before.

The cars were parked under the trees facing west, ready to go. The first in line was an ambulance.

The refugees were restless and extremely nervous, and the time went on and on without anything happening. The evening was a long time coming that day. People were growing more and more hysterical. Until then we had calmed them by saying that we had to wait for darkness. But now it was dark.

My friend Jack, who later ended up in the Dachau concentration camp and with whom I had spent many wonderful hours during the past year working for the illegal press, asked me to go down to the beach with him and wait for the ship. We were waiting for a signal light from the sea... The arrangement was that the boat, when at anchor, would signal an A, and we would answer with a BD.

Finally a light blinked. We could not quite agree whether it was an A, but we decided that those idiots probably had forgotten what an A looked like. And Jack answered by blinking BD. Immediately a searchlight was turned on and swept across the beach. Jack and I threw ourselves down on the ground. My memory of what happened next is very chaotic. I raced up to the cottage and into the adjoining stable and announced that we had to leave. I must have run pretty fast, for I shot past the whole convoy and came right up to the ambulance in front.

Something occurred which I recall with great shame and embarrassment. But then again, things like that do happen when you are young and have never been taught to think right – and at the same time are thoroughly shaken by what you have just been through.

Someone handed me a pistol, an old revolver, and so help me God, if I did not accept it, saying, "yes, sir!" I then took up position on the running board of the first ambulance, and off we went. I was filled with a crazy sense of heroism, rushing through the forest with twigs and dry leaves slapping against my face.

We ended up in a ranger's house belonging to the Gjorslev Estate where all the old and sick people were put up. Eighty of the youngest ones were sent to a pavillion near the beach. The taxis were sent away to the manor house and the ambulances were sent home. By now there was near-total panic.

At some point I was talking politics with another helper, a young man wearing a white shirt and a bow tie. I was sure that he was a DSU (Danish Social Democratic Youth) in conflict with his party. He was the first one ever to say to me, "We shall have to find a way of cooperating with you communists."

I was very proud that he could tell I was a communist. We met again many years later, and he, Jørgen Vedel Petersen, claims that he was not at all a Social Democrat but a Trotskyite.

I cannot quite recall how the afternoon passed, but a sinister gloom descended on us all. When darkness fell, we were sent off, first some private cars, then ambulances with the weakest people. The rest left in small groups or on cattle trucks. Spaced far apart and by odd routes, we drove from Gjorslev to the island of Møn in the course of a few hours. At crucial points along the way, helpers from the University Rifles Club were posted with lanterns and signal flags. On Møn we came to a very small harbor, which I have since found out must have been Klintholm harbor, where there was a large, brick barn.

Several hours would go by between the arrivals of the various groups. The refugees were placed in the drafty brick barn. We almost did not dare show ourselves there. (28)

THE MAN AND THE MECHANICAL PENCIL

At three o'clock in the morning the last cattle truck finally arrived. It had been four hours under way. We rushed over to open it and get the people out. The first person to jump into my arms was one of the men from the University Rifles Club. He grabbed hold of me and started dancing, saying it felt good to be back among white men, for by God, it was awful to be locked up with those Jews.

I have never in my life bawled anyone out as I did him. I still get a white-hot sensation in my brain when I think of it. It is strange how – when you experience so many powerful and violent things – some tiny detail will stick in your mind.

The refugees were sick and had thrown up and wet their pants. They were frightened to death. Families had been split up, luggage was lost and there was no end to the misery. On top of that we were on Møn, caught in a trap.

When everyone was out of the cattle truck, a small man, a tailor by the name of Nachum, suddenly became hysterical.

His wife had disappeared. It turned out that she had been sent back to Copenhagen with a case of appendicitis. She came to Sweden a week later. His children were missing. We later found them crying in a corner of the brick barn. He had even had to leave his luggage behind somewhere.

But now he had lost his fountain pen, and he refused to leave the truck until he had retrieved it. It had to be found. The driver wanted to leave. The riflemen were cursing. When some day I stand at the Pearly Gates and have to come up with something that will make up for all my sins, I really think it speaks in my favor that I suddenly realized that for him this was serious. There were limits to what a human being could bear to lose.

I jumped onto the truck and in a few minutes we found it, with a silk pompom at the end of it. His luck had turned, and he immediately used the pen to write down his name and address for me. That is how I know his name was Nachum and that he was a tailor.

At the time, this ship was called "Sølyst." It ferried Jews to Sweden from the waters around Gjorslev and Stevns. In the early 70s, the ship was called "Fri" (Free) and was a floating commune.

Professor Ege had got hold of a ship. The plan was that it would enter the harbor when everyone had arrived safely. It had been waiting out at sea for several hours. The wind and the current were rough. Three times the skipper tried to maneuver the ship into the harbor, but it veered off. On the fourth try he did something very impressive: He throttled to full speed, aiming the boat right at the pier – and that way the current made it drift just enough to let it slip through the mouth of the harbor. We moved the people onto the ship like greased lightning. The hatches to the hold were shut, and in less than a quarter of an hour all the refugees were on board. The skipper cast off the moorings and set off.

Afterwards we were told that the ship took five hours to reach the Swedish coast.

The helpers were driven to Bispebjerg Hospital. First we were given morning coffee and cigarettes. Then we remembered that we had not eaten for several days and were given soup and meatballs. Afterwards we had a bath and got into some clean underwear. And then we went to a bar.

A whole day and a night went by before we started in again. (28)

FOUR GIRLS

Four girls played an important part in the shipping of the Jews: Elsebeth Kieler, 25 years old; Ebba Lund, 20; her sister, Ulla Lund, 19; and Henny Sinding Sundø, 22.

It is impossible to know just how many Jews their organization brought across The Sound; no one kept track, but it amounted to several hundred in the course of October and November. Their job was to see to the expedition of the "goods" handed over to them by "export companies." They picked up Jews from their apartments, from parks and forests, from backyards and stairways, and from non-Jewish friends with whom they had sought refuge.

Elsebeth Kieler was a university student. Her two brothers, Jørgen and Flemming, who were studying medicine, were among the founders of the resistance organization called "Holger Danske" and were captured by the Germans and sent south to a concentration camp. They survived, came back as human skeletons, but recovered. After the war, they continued their studies and had long careers as physicians.

Jørgen relates:

> On Wednesday, September 29, it became clear to the Jewish community that the situation was serious, and the Jews began to leave their homes. Soon we were hearing about the first suicides.

The official confirmation of the pogroms came on Thursday, September 30.

There was a widespread feeling of indignation and despair, and the university students immediately declared a strike.

The need for escape routes was acute. We came into contact with Professor Richard Ege. At the same time we had plans of starting our own route.

This became possible when Elsebeth and Klaus Rønholt, in the course of the weekend – October 3 and 4 – managed to collect a small fortune, and their plan was realized when Ebba Lund established the North Harbor route. (29)

That weekend Elsebeth and Klaus had gone by taxi from one estate to the next to collect money to finance the escape of the Jews. One thousand kroner was the price of a "Jewish ticket," as they called it.

At one place, the Gavnø Estate, they happened to arrive in the middle of an evening affair. The incident is described by Elsebeth:

> We made our way to the main building through the kitchen area. From there we came up into the house until we suddenly found ourselves at a large dinner party. "You handle the ladies," Klaus said, and steered towards the parlor where the gentlemen were.
>
> It was probably naive of us to drive around and entrust our secret undertakings to all those people. But in a strange way our naiveté was our strength then. It disarmed people. Klaus knew more or less all the people we visited. Or at least they knew his family. Klaus in fact deserves the credit for this tour which was all his doing.

(Klaus Rønholt was later captured by the Germans. He died on November 22, 1944, in the Husum forced-labor camp in southern Schleswig, a "subsidiary" of the Neuengamme concentration camp.)

One Million Kroner Collected

They managed to collect one million kroner. (Translated into 1993 money, this corresponds to 20 million kroner – or about $3 million.)

Elsebeth comments:

> It may serve for comparison that after the tour I had two envelopes hidden in my bureau at home: One held the million for the transportation of the Jews, the other held a month's allowance from my parents – 20 kroner for myself.

During the occupation, she was known as the girl in the red beret. Her real name is Ebba Lund, and until 1993 she was a professor at the Copenhagen Agricultural College. She organized an escape route leaving from Copenhagen's North Harbor. Later, when the North Harbor became too risky, these activities were moved to the South Harbor.

Ebba Lund undertook negotiations with the fishermen and established the North Harbor route. It left from Skudehavnen, north of the Free Port in Copenhagen.

"When the transportation of the Jews began, I, like so many others, wracked my brains for ways to come up with shipping contacts and money," recounts Ebba Lund, who today is retired from the Royal Veterinary and Agricultural University in Copenhagen, where she was an international and esteemed professor of Virology. In resistance circles Ebba Lund was known as "the girl with the red beret."

> Elsebeth and Klaus had managed to collect quite a lot of money, whereas Ulla (my sister) and I went begging for money, large and small amounts, wherever we could. After a while people would come to our home to donate money.
>
> Our first contact in the North Harbor was an oddball called "the American" who lived in a shed and owned a small boat. Soon a fisherman and some others became involved. I was in the crazy situation of having more than enough boating capacity. About a dozen boats were willing to sail regularly. Some passengers were troublesome, insisting on wearing several layers of coats and bringing large amounts of luggage. Others, who perhaps had more experience of life, more of a perspective on things and better nerves, were exceptionally easy to work with. (29)

Ebba Lund recalls one particular morning when one of "her" fishermen told her that they had found a barge adrift on The Sound, filled with people. It had happened in the evening, and the fishermen had brought them along to the North Harbor. The wretched people were put up in the fishermen's sheds for the night. They were without money. They had been helped by another transport organization, which had put them in contact with a fisherman who, for a fee, had taken them in tow on a barge. When they were well out of the harbor, he had cut the rope, abandoning the floating barge.

Later on Ebba Lund gave up using the North Harbor. It had become too unsafe. She moved her organization to the South Harbor. She became so confident that a couple of times she shipped off refugees from Gammel Strand, right in the center of Copenhagen, at midday. (30)

The fourth of the girls who made a great contribution in those days was Henny Sinding Sundø. She was employed by the Lighthouse Department, where her father was the chief. The Department's boat, "Gerda III," brought provisions to the Drogden lighthouse and placed buoys along the three-mile limit off the Danish coast.

"GERDA III" – THE ROUTE FROM WILDER'S SQUARE

Henny Sinding Sundø recalls:

One of the first days in October I was called down to the "Gerda III," which was moored right in front of the Lighthouse Storage. When I came on board, all of the four crew members were gathered, looking quite serious. They did not usually look that way, but before long the explanation came. They had decided that the "Gerda III" would be ideal for transporting Jewish refugees to Sweden. She had permission to sail as far as the three-mile limit and had to go out to the Drogden Lighthouse every day anyway. The crew had planned it all, but they still felt that they needed some sort of "unofficial permission" from the management. It would be a bit difficult for them to just steal the boat for this purpose. Luckily, my father happened to be the boss of the whole business. The end result of our conversation was that I would square things with "the old man."

I asked my father straight off not to institute a search for the "Gerda III" and not to blame the crew if the boat did not always stick to its usual course. I also asked my father to arrange a berth for the "Gerda III" on Christianshavn's Canal across from Wilder's Square...

I promised him that the boat would perform its daily chores, though perhaps slightly off-schedule.

I actually think that my father was glad to have his department involved in assisting in the transportation of refugees.

In this way the "Gerda III" began working as a refugee-transport vessel manned by skipper Tønnesen, engineer Hansen ("Sparky"), Steffensen ("Stef") and Andersen.

Now a hectic period began. All five of us had heard of an awful lot of Jews who needed to get across The Sound in a hurry. It was arranged so that each refugee, accompanied by no more than one child, was told to show up at a certain time and place. Here, one of us would arrive and take the refugee to Strand Street, where we had secured the assistance of kind, helpful people whom we could trust. Often the refugees would have to wait here for a couple of days. If possible, we preferred to bring married couples with children across at the same time. It was sometimes difficult to solve this mathematical problem.

To prevent informers from getting on board, we had to be careful about which refugees we contacted and with whom they stayed. If even one wrong person were to find out about the "Gerda III" route, it would be useless forever after, and the department would be in deep trouble.

At the end of Strand Street we had borrowed a warehouse (Justesen's Storage). On the Strand Street side there was a door through which we could enter quickly. On the other side was a gate opening onto the pier, just in front of the place where the "Gerda III" was moored. Each night I could manage to pick up 15 people. There was not room for more than that on board.

It was our unbelievable luck that we never met any Germans in Strand Street at night.

Our big headache was two German guards who patrolled the pier outside the warehouse, continuously walking back and forth. They would meet right in front of the "Gerda III," turn around, march 100 meters in opposite directions, turn around and meet up again right in front of the "Gerda III." This was hair-raising, since we had to make use of the exact moment when they had faced each other, had turned around, and were walking away from each other with their backs to the boat.

One at a time, the Jews had to dash across the few meters between the warehouse and the boat, where they were helped on board and immediately jammed into the hold. And when all the adults were on board, we brought the children...

It is incredible that the Germans never turned around and looked. They could not possibly help hearing that someone was running across the cobblestones.

With 15 people packed tightly into the hold, the "Gerda III" was ready for departure. We all said a silent prayer, for as soon as "Sparky"

"Will we get across this evening?" is the title of this painting from 1952. It is signed K.F.J. The artist is unknown. It depicts Jews, hidden in a barn in Snekkersten, waiting to leave for Sweden.

started up the engine, two guards immediately appeared. Every morning they had to come on board to check that everything was in order.

They must either have been nice Germans or else very sleepy, for they never asked to have the gear on top of the hatch removed to see what was hidden below. But then the crew would also quite often and quite willingly hand them a good-morning beer.

Then the "Gerda III" took to the sea, officially going to the Drogden Lighthouse, but along the way making a sidetrip to the Swedish coast where she got the refugees safely ashore before setting course for the Drogden Lighthouse.

I would stand in the warehouse and watch the boat cast off, then quickly make my way home in the early morning.

My parents never said anything, neither when I left at night nor when I arrived home in the morning. My poor mother. To leave the house I had to go through her bedroom. She would hear me tiptoeing out every night, but only drew further into her covers, pretending not to know. My thanks to Mother.(30)

A Jew helped into the hold of a fishing vessel.

SHIPPED OFF FROM NYHAVN

The theater director Sam Besekow did not try to escape right away. He believed he was safe, because he was married to a non-Jew. He relates:

> One morning in November, I met the playwright Kjeld Abell on Gammel Kongevej. This was in 1943. He happened to see me from the opposite pavement and, with some hesitation, crossed the street and came up to me:
> – You are here?
> – Yes, where else?
> – You can't walk around here in broad daylight with that face of yours!
> – How... ?
> – You should be in Sweden.
> – Not on my life.
> – On your life, yes... you are endangering all the rest of us.
> – But...
> And that is when Henny and I went underground, as it was called.
> We found ourselves an apartment in a basement on Klampenborg Road, just across from the race track, staying with a family named Rosenstand.

Mrs. Rosenstand was German, a real little *Hausmütterchen,* and not just playing the part. But, even though she was German, in the midst of those German days, she was so very Danish... We spent our days in that basement until we were told that it was time to leave.

Everything was hush-hush and oh-so-secret, and late one evening a closed van was waiting outside. In true Danish film-comedy style, we stole from the front door of the house to the garden gate and from there to the car door. It slammed shut behind us, and we sat there, totally in the dark, unable at all to see where we were going or how. We blindly tried to guess where the "rescuers" would unload us – north, south. In the pitch-black darkness it was impossible to get a sense of direction.

– Leave it to them, they must know what they are doing...

– Yes, but...

Mistakes had happened. How many were captured that time in the Gilleleje Church? One drunken informer and one overly zealous Gestapo man had been enough to make things go wrong.

– Down south it is safe – still. Down around Køge, I have heard that there is a regular migration, people marching through the streets wearing several layers of fur coats and carrying huge suitcases. And no one even lifts an eyebrow. It would be very easy just to lift the receiver – and they'd have you! – But no... This is Denmark...

– All that is very well, but from which shore are they planning to ship us, I wonder?...

– I have a feeling it will be from Snekkersten. That is where Gersfelt, Jørgen, my old schoolmate lives... Do you remember when he and I, right after our graduation, went bicycling to Paris... the world was all bright and shiny – and all evil belonged to a distant past. We looked at Verdun and the Grave of the Bayonets as if we were looking at museum pieces... and yet this was only twelve years after the 1918 Peace Treaty.

A Film that Had to be Finished

Here I sit, hidden behind my typewriter, reminding myself that we are now in 1993. Fifty years have gone by – and it is still as if we were right in the middle of that hell...

I remember the moment when the car began to slow down, brakes, silence, steps, the door opening – where were we?

Director Sam Besekow didn't leave until he had conducted the final scene of a crime-comedy in which he appeared together with the actor Gunnar Lauring. That's Besekow with his hands up.

I do not think I had ever really understood the word "surprised" until that moment:

There was no mistaking it. It was the studio of the Palladium film company in the suburb of Hellerup. We were taken inside, into the studio, and with a sinking feeling saw The Sound lying out there behind us.

Why were we here? Were we to wait for a ship in the Hellerup harbor, or... ? From Køge and Stege everyone had left on a schooner. Here we could not see even the paddle of a kayak. The large hall was enveloped in twilight, the gates were closed, the windows shuttered. But we were able to make out the presence of the film director Johan Jacobsen and the light technician... and the set. At that point, of course, I realized what it was all about: *While the Lawyer Sleeps*, a crime comedy in which I played – and soon was made-up to look like – a terrible Chinese gangster.

This film had to be finished before I could go to Sweden. It was not possible to edit the film until the final scene between Gunnar Lauring and myself had been shot, a scene in which I – pistol in hand and firing several loud shots – threaten the lawyer to... I do not remember what.

Gunnar Lauring was sleeping safely in his bed at home. His part had already been shot and was to be inserted between the pistol shots and the shots of me alone. I am afraid of gunshots and caused a whole roll of film to be ruined.

Each time the shot sounded, I would shut my eyes tightly. A little while later I really shut my eyes – this was no longer play. Steps could be heard outside, what now? Gestapo? Goodbye Sweden, ye country old and free... There was a rattling of keys. The small side door slid open, and standing there was the head of Palladium Films, Svend Nielsen. He nodded knowingly:

"I know you will be gone in a few hours after you have finished this. I have contacted Doctor Dymling in Stockholm. You will be employed by the Swedish Film Industry and will be receiving a monthly salary for as long as you are there. You do not have to do anything for the money, not any more than what you absolutely want to do. And here is a hundred dollars to compensate you for having suffered these first few days."

That was Denmark in those days.

The refugee ships that sailed in October were jam-packed. It was as if the ghostly fleet of The Flying Dutchman were sailing through the dark of night.

Leaving so late, in November, we had the privilege of being the only couple on board. We lay huddled in the foetal position in two herring crates that were nailed shut – and the place from which we were shipped was the safest place in Denmark: Nyhavn Canal, right under the noses of the German officers in their headquarters at the Hotel d'Angleterre.

The Gestapo came on board in the grey of early morning. Either they really did not suspect anything, or else they pretended not to. It is hard to say; there was so much funny business going on in those days. We set out at a steady pace, a fishing boat going about its business. Well clear of the coast, we headed directly for Sweden. At the sound of a speedboat approaching, the fishermen turned off the engine. The crates were opened, and we were able to stretch our backs, blinked into the morning sunlight and into a glass of sparkling champagne: WELCOME TO SWEDEN.

On shore, in Barsebäck, a dear couple stood waiting, weeping and holding hands: my father and mother, who had been told that their son had been shot.

And the police were there, also waiting. For Henny and me.

To say I was spoiled would be putting it mildly. Always and everywhere there was someone there for me when things were difficult. In this case it was the Swedish police who put me on a train to Stockholm, where I was received by the writers Brita von Horn and Moberg. They installed me in von Horn's apartment in 28 Hamngatan with a maid who each morning brought us our coffee with a curtsey and on the second day handed me a manuscript: Sune Bergström's *Less of Morality*, a wild farce, which was not made less wild by being produced at the Swedish Drama Studio. It was staged 24 times at various Stockholm theaters and at the National Theater. Yes, I was probably the most privileged refugee in those years. Is it really 50 years ago – or was it yesterday? (31)

MOSS FROM SÆBY

Some fishermen and members of the resistance ended up paying for their efforts to help by spending a long time in prison. Some died.

Among them was the innkeeper of Snekkersten, Henry Thomsen, who died on December 4, 1944, in the Neuengamme concentration camp.

Kalle Moss got off alive. He died at age 75 last year, and has written about his experiences during the occupation. His ship was named "Karen," after his wife. One day in 1943, when Kalle told her that he now and then sailed illegally to Sweden, she answered, "Of course you must take those who need it across."

At that time she had just become pregnant with their first child.

Moss sailed Jews and members of the resistance across until he was arrested by the Gestapo in January 1945. On her way back from Sweden, the "Karen" would carry guns and explosives for the resistance movement.

Some Fishermen Went to Prison

Five o'clock in the morning we were wakened by the sound of snowballs being thrown at our window. Someone shouted, "Kalle, I have to talk to you" – and I knew then that it was all over. To Karen I said, "It is the Germans. Don't worry, I think I'll just have to go with them to the harbor. They probably want to check whether we have anybody on board, but we don't." Whether she believed me, I don't know, but at any rate she was calm.

I then went down and opened the front door, wearing only pajamas, and right away a soldier stuck a machine gun into my stomach. Another one was pointing a pistol at me. In German they shouted, *"Sind Sie Carl Rasmussen?"* "Yes," I answered and said, "Take it easy," in Danish. They must have understood, for they calmed down and accompanied me upstairs.

Karen was sitting in bed looking rather frightened, of course. They asked, "Is it true that you have nothing on board?"

"Nothing," I said. "It won't be long before you see me again, sweetheart."

The two soldiers searched the small apartment thoroughly. One of them was very interested in the radio. "Do you have a pistol?" they asked. "No," I said, flinging out my hands, "go ahead and search." It was a good thing that I had refused when Jørgen Blær made me the offer.

When I had dressed, one of them pointed to Karen and then looked at me. "Goodbye," he muttered in Danish. "I'll pray for you," said Karen, this small, brave person, who did not cry, and raised my spirits with "I love you." I now realized that she did not believe that I just had to go on board.

When I came into the living-room, one of the Germans had a pair of handcuffs ready. Another grabbed my arms and was going to pull them around my back. I do not know why, but something must have told me that this would be uncomfortable, and I wriggled out of his grip. I was young and strong and he was not very big. I placed my hands in front of me and said in my bad English, "laying on of hands." This they must have understood, for they laughed and said yes, yes. For the first and hopefully the last time I had been handcuffed. I had to wear the handcuffs from five o'clock in the morning until ten o'clock at night, because the one who had the keys to my handcuffs was off duty when we arrived at the jail in the town of Aalborg...

When I was taken into the basement and said "Good morning," one of the Danes, giving me a kick, shouted "Shut up." So it was probably a good thing that I was wearing those handcuffs. It gave me a good excuse, at least to myself, not to sock him one. But I probably would not have done that anyway.

Then my name was called, and I was escorted upstairs. There, at a table, sat two men. The first one called himself "Reinar" (a cover name). His real name was Jessen Mikkelsen, a Danish prison guard. I do not remember the name of the other one. There were several Danes, each of them a hell of a guy, in his own opinion. There were also several Germans.

"Reinar" conducted the brief interrogation. Some rubber truncheons and a wet towel had been laid out, while he himself held a gun in his hand. He said, "You might as well confess and tell the truth, for we have the means of making you talk," which I could see for myself. "You have sailed refugees to Sweden and brought weapons and explosives back with you to Denmark. Right?"

"Some of it is right," I said. "We have sailed some Danes to Varberg; we have not brought weapons and explosives home with us, only some packages containing bicycle tires and other things that have been unavailable to us here for several years."

"You're lying," he roared, picking up a truncheon and slamming it down on the table. "How many Jews have you sailed across and how many saboteurs?"

"I don't know," I answered. He reeled off some names, asking if I knew any of them – including the names of some of the people now sitting in the basement. I could not deny knowing these, of course. Then more names, Poul Larsen from Frederikshavn. "That person I have never seen." "That doesn't matter, we've got him," he answered.

There were more people he wanted to find out about, and since I knew that they were in Sweden, I could admit to these. Then my first interrogation was over. To say that I was not afraid would not be quite truthful, but I certainly was extremely annoyed...

Jews were hidden in this hut while waiting to escape.

Why I got off without being beaten up, I do not know. Several of the others had been. When we had all been interrogated, we were taken into a bus, to the accompaniment of Danish curses and the German *"los, los"* (off, off). We were of course anxious to find out where we were going. I figured it was Aalborg. It was forbidden for us prisoners to talk. It was infuriating to listen to these Danish traitors who were laughing at us. There were five Germans and five Danes sitting there with their machine guns. Herman and I sat together just behind the driver, a Dane.

When we came to the road going into Aalborg, he drove straight through town and continued to Frederikshavn, where we stopped at Kragholmen at a large (confiscated) villa. After a while, more prisoners came out. They were unknown to me then, but I got to know them in the course of the following months. The minister, Rev. Hanhøj, another minister, Rev. Vestergaard, the chauffeur, Nygård, and three or four others. So now the bus was filled and we drove south again.

When we re-entered Sæby it was nine o'clock in the evening. There were people in the streets, and it was a bitter experience to sit in a bus as a prisoner and see others pass by as free men. We saw how the brutal Danish traitors were hollering and singing with the Germans. When we drove past the place where we lived, I looked up at our windows and thought of Karen. At that moment I felt regret. But then I thought of what Karen had said earlier: "...those who need to get across." (33)

SEEN FROM SWEDEN

The municipal health officer in Höganäs, H.C. Widding, tells how he experienced the arrival of the refugees in Sweden. He was keeping a diary at the time. Here are his notations from Friday, October 8:

Refugees arrive in Sweden. Some were housed by family and friends, though most went to refugee camps. Danish schools were established with teachers recruited from the refugees. Schoolbooks were imported illegally by the Danish-Swedish Refugee Service.

I shall not forget the night between the 8th and 9th of October. I had fallen asleep around twelve-thirty, when the police phoned to inform me that 124 refugees had arrived at the harbor. I quickly got dressed and mobilized the Red Cross people... Among others, we received Adolph Meyer, head doctor at a children's hospital in Copenhagen.

Meyer had celebrated his 72nd birthday on September 29. As was customary, cake and champagne had been served at the hospital. In the morning he received a message from the Medical Association that he had to leave immediately. He was to bring only nightwear and 10,000 – 15,000 Danish kroner. He had to pay 10,000 for his passage across. Those who had money had to pay for those who were poor...

Meyer had been hunted like a wild animal. No novel could describe what he had been through... Once he was hiding in a hayloft along with 80 others when the Gestapo came. They searched the stable where six horses had been heard kicking. At first they forgot the hayloft, but they returned. A minute and a half before they came back, Meyer and several of the others managed to get away in some cars. The rest had to hide somewhere nearby.

Families were split up, and it was heartrending to hear a mother crying because she could not find her son and two young daughters. I was glad when three days later the three children were delivered to me. I was able to tell them that their parents were already in Höganäs. Some [of the refugees] had left their children in Denmark with people who had offered to help.

The longing they felt for their children was agonizing. Some people would react by laughing and grinning when they had come ashore.

The refugees would sing the Danish or Swedish national anthem as they sailed into Höganäs Harbor. It was very moving. Many of the children did not understand why they had to flee. They were Danish, of course, and had never given it a thought that they were also Jewish.

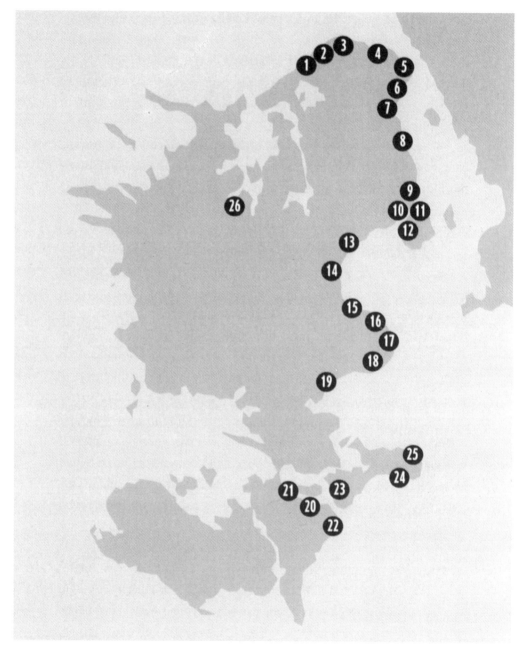

There were 26 embarkation points on Zealand, between Udsholt north of Gilleleje (3) and Hesnæs (22). The most important escape routes originated from Gilleleje, Helsingør-Humlebæk, Strøby-Gjorslev and Copenhagen Harbor. It is estimated that 200-300 vessels were engaged in transporting refugees. (32)

GOOD GERMANS

Either they must have been good Germans or else they were very sleepy, says Henny Sinding Sundø of the German guards who walked back and forth in front of the "Gerda III." They pretended not to see what was happening right behind their backs.

Many Germans did behave decently. Without them it would not have been possible to transport more than 7,000 Jews from their homes to the coast between Smidstrup, north of Gilleleje, and Hesnæs, from where the refugee boats left. It would have been very easy for the Germans to catch more Jews in their net. The rescue operations lasted a couple of months, but most of the refugees got across The Sound in the course of the first two weeks.

The Germans could have stopped and searched the coastal trains, an escape route which many Jews used to get from Copenhagen to places along the coast. The latter would have been easy prey for the German police. They did not look like people going on a vacation but had "refugee" written all over their faces.

But there are no reports that the Germans searched the coastal trains. Hundreds of Jews were transported from the Copenhagen hospitals to the train station in Valby, where they bought a return ticket to Køge. As if the trick of buying a return trip would fool anybody. Everybody knew that they were on the run. Yet, also in these cases the Germans did not intervene.

It was without enthusiasm that the German powers-that-be in Denmark obeyed the order from Germany that Danish Jews must now be treated like all other European Jews and deported.

There were some zealous Germans here and there who did their best to capture Jews. The most fanatic were the Danish Nazis who served as support troops to the Germans.

Whether it is right to speak of good Germans, as Henny Sinding Sundø does, is hard to say, but there are many reports of Germans acting decently during the persecution of the Jews in Denmark. The Danish Jews were exempted from the Nazi rule that Jews had to be exterminated. It is difficult to give a satisfactory explanation. Some were against the actions taken against the Jews, some were indifferent. It looked as if Germany was about to lose the war, so why not let the Jews get away. Some were afraid of encountering armed members of the resistance who were escorting the refugees. Some were bribed with money or liquor to turn their backs, so as not to see what was happening around them.

The physician Jørgen Gersfelt tells of an incident when a suspicious-looking garbage truck was stopped by a patrol of German soldiers in Helsingør.

The soldiers raised the lid… but when they saw that the truck was full of Jews, the sergeant exclaimed, "Abraham, Isaac and Jacob." Then they slammed the lid back down, laughing, and let the truck pass. (11)

Ebba Lund tells of another episode when German soldiers preferred not to get involved:

> We had gotten some passengers into a boat (in the South Harbor). The engines were already running, when a German patrol came down the path between the sheds and out onto the pier. I went to stand very close to a brawny fisherman and tried as best I could to look romantic. The Germans did not say anything but stood still, looking. They looked at the policemen who were carrying pistols and had a determined air. Then they looked at the fishermen, there was about a dozen of them. (There were only five German soldiers.) They also looked at me. Then

they turned around and left. I am absolutely convinced that they knew what was going on. But they realized they would pay for it dearly if they started interfering.

Erik Stenersen, a member of the Holger Danske resistance group, relates:

> Fourteen refugees were captured by the German coast artillery on the Zealand Point. I had been helping to hide them in some summer houses when we were surprised by the Germans. Hidden in a ditch, I witnessed their arrest, and after the war was able to testify against a Danish informer. We could do nothing when the refugees were taken to the Nyborg jail by the Germans. A little later a bus with "German" insignia showed up and picked up the refugees without anyone protesting. The German soldiers apparently preferred not to get mixed up in anything. In this way the Jews were freed again. After the war the informer was sent to jail for four years. (35)

A member of the resistance, Kaj Christiansen, writes:

> The Germans set about stopping the refugee-traffic in a vague and halfhearted manner... It is likely that there was a considerable number of Germans, not least in the Wehrmacht, who were against the persecution of the Danish Jews. They tolerated their escape and even sabotaged efforts to stop them. (36)

John Saietz recounts:

> In order not to call attention to ourselves, we had arranged that we would walk singly or in pairs to where we were to meet on the beach, a short distance from Snekkersten harbor.
>
> My father went alone, carrying a small suitcase. When he arrived at our meeting place, he was quite upset. He told us that on the way he had run into a German officer. Panicking, he had tried to get rid of

the suitcase without the officer noticing it in the semi-darkness. The officer had told him, *"Ruhig, ich tue Ihnen nichts."* (Take it easy, I won't harm you.) (37)

The Germans' Lack of Enthusiasm

Leo Igelski tells another story of the Germans' lack of enthusiasm. This time it had to do with two Gestapo people.

> The Igelski family were put up at an estate near Orehoved. "A local village idiot" informed on the place, and on October 19, two Gestapo people arrived at the Orehoved train station, asking directions to a certain forest.
>
> The station master was wondering what the Gestapo wanted at that address and directed them to another forest nearby. Then he called the owner of the correct forest and told him of the Gestapo inquiry. The lord of the manor thanked him without revealing anything. But he quickly let us know that we were no longer safe at the estate.
>
> In the meantime, the Gestapo men had reached the wrong forest. When they did not find our house, they immediately drove back to Copenhagen, without making inquiries elsewhere or returning to Orehoved.

Apparently the whole German machine was prepared to have the raid fail. The most obedient and horribly efficient police organization in the world at that time let itself be stopped by a wrong address. Why and how was this possible? (38)

And here is a German testimony:

> In the days when the persecution of the Jews broke out in Denmark, a German ship was positioned between Helsingør and Helsingborg. The ship's captain and the radio officer were both anti-Nazi. The radio

officer began transmitting on the radio frequency of the German harbor police, preventing them from sending or receiving on that frequency.

Shortly thereafter the German patrol boat located the ship, and a man boarded it.

"Was machen Sie?" (What are you doing?), he gruffly asked. The radio officer replied that the ship's radio was out of order and that he was sorry about the disturbance.

This was his and the captain's contribution to a neutralization of the German harbor police's efforts, and thus to the rescue of the Danish Jews. (39)

The German chief of shipping in Århus was named Friedrich Wilhelm Lübke. While he was visiting Berlin in September 1943, friends at headquarters informed him of the planned persecution of the Danish Jews.

Shortly after his return to Århus he was ordered to prepare the ship "Monte Rosa" for transportation of the Danish Jews. The name of the ship's captain was Heinrich Bertram. He and Lübke were friends.

They refused to participate in the action against the Jews, stating that the "Monte Rosa" was not available due to engine failure.

In 1969, Lübke became Prime Minister of Schleswig-Holstein. His brother was Heinrich Lübke, the Federal President of Germany from 1959 to 1969. (40)

There was a widespread German unwillingness to have the persecutions succeed. These examples are only a small selection of the many reports of German soldiers who turned their backs. The same was true of the people in the German navy.

The question is whether this indifference was encouraged by the top ranks of the German occupation force. Did all the Germans who failed to do their duty know that they did not risk accusations of negligence?

Or was the German attitude as spontaneous and improvised as the Danish rescue operation? It is possible.

GERMAN HELPERS

There are also accounts of Germans directly helping refugee Jews.

In one case a German platoon came marching into Skovshoved Harbor and sealed off the area. Some refugees were hiding behind a shed, waiting to get away.

Shortly after, a couple of cars arrived at the harbor, and about ten Jews emerged. The Germans saw to it that these people got into a boat that was waiting for them. When it was well out of the harbor, the Germans left.

Before leaving, the German officer told the Danish coast guard on patrol, "I was only able to do this because I know that there is not a single Nazi in my platoon."

Some refugees are said to have been brought to safety by a German speedboat. Rumor has it that the German captain approached a Danish acquaintance and offered to bring Jewish refugees to Sweden.

The German boat took them to the middle of The Sound and hailed some approaching Swedish vessels.

The Germans put lifebelts on the Jews and threw them into the water, where they were picked up by the Swedes.

On the night of October 1-2, the Germans came to No. 37 Main Street in the suburb of Søborg to pick up a Jewish carpenter named K. Kvetny and his wife.

They found no one home. The Danish informer suggested, "Let's go upstairs, his son lives there." "No," said the Germans. "He is not on our list." (41)

A similar incident took place the same night in Frederiksberg, where the paternal uncle of the former Chief Rabbi, Bent Melchior, was living in the same building as his sister. She was employed by a non-Jewish family. The Germans came to pick up the uncle but did not find him home. They asked the caretaker if he knew where Melchior was. The reply was negative. "His sister works for the X family, ask her."

The Germans looked her up. She denied having any knowledge of her brother's whereabouts. As she was not on the Germans' list of arrests, she was let off with no further ado. (42)

The flight of the Danish Jews would never have been so successful if it had not been for Germans who either sabotaged the persecution of Jews or remained passive. No one has systematically examined this side of the story. Here is an example: Max Mauff was a high-ranking German officer during the occupation of Denmark. He was a colonel and the commandant of Copen-hagen. On August 24, 1991, I received a letter from his daughter in Hamburg. She wrote that her father died in 1977. He told her that he had helped Jews escape to Sweden. After the war, he became the director of a Jewish company in Regensburg. "Since my father was a professional soldier, with no business experience, I must assume that he got this position as a reward for his efforts on behalf of the Danish Jews during the war." It is not so strange that a daughter would like to think well of her father, so she cannot be considered a reliable witness.

The same year, on November 24, I received a letter from a Dane called Walter Kienitz. He was originally German, a soldier in the German army during World War II, but a member of a religious anti-Nazi opposition group. He moved to Denmark after the war and lives in Nyborg. Kienitz writes of the Germans who either directly or indirectly contributed to the failure of the anti-Jewish action. He mentions Colonel Max Mauff as a very correct officer of the old Kaiser school in Germany.

Kienitz mentions that in the early 1960s, Mauff was in Hornbæk, where he visited some friends from the time of the occupation – retired Police Inspector Svend Gredsted and his wife. During his stay, Kienitz recounts, Mauff was visited by three Danish Jews who came to thank him for his personal efforts during the action against the Jews. Kienitz refers me to Gredsted's wife. By telephone, Mrs. Gredsted confirms the story. She remembers that Mauff was late for an appointment at the Gredsted home. He said that he had been delayed by some Danish Jews who had come to thank him.

Gredsted was appointed by the Commisioner of the Copenhagen Police to be liaison officer to the German occupational authorities, represented by Max Mauff. The episode concerning the Jews who came to thank Mauff and the fact that he was hired after the war by a Jewish company in Regensburg tend to confirm the daughter's story.

Unfortunately, it is too late to investigate this and other similar stories. The main characters are dead. For many years after the war, we hung onto a black-and-white picture of Germans as being all bad. They were collectively responsible for what happened during the Nazi period and World War II. Now, when we can view things from a distance and feel able to make evaluations in a less prejudiced way, it is too late.

THE BLOODHOUND OF PARIS

One thing is certain. If the Jews had not been warned in time, many more would have been arrested when the German trucks with the green police troops drove through the city on the night of October 1-2, 1943.

Doctor Werner Best

The warning came from the top rank of the German occupying power, from the Reich-appointed Gestapo man and SS general, Doctor Werner Best. He played a fantastic, double-dealing game which saved our lives, as well as his own.

One of the most inexplicable episodes in the history of the Danish occupation is why Best decided that the Jews should be given a chance to escape. Best was no friend of the Jews. He had been a Nazi since his youth.

He came to Denmark on November 5, 1942, with the reputation of being brutal and merciless toward Hitler's enemies. "The Bloodhound of Paris," he was called.

The man had psychopathic tendencies. After the war, Best was placed in a Danish prison and examined by psychiatrists. The medical report on his state of mind stated, among other things, that he was a self-asserting and ambitious person, given to indulgence in self-pity and egocentricity. He was "a psychopath to a minor or moderate degree, of the self-assertive type."

This was the man Adolf Hitler had sent to Denmark to govern "that ridiculous country," as Best was to call Denmark later at a meeting with the editors-in-chief of the Danish newspapers. (44)

As it turned out, this man was not the worst choice as Hitler's governor in occupied Denmark, neither from a Danish nor from a German point of view.

If Best had not come to Denmark, but had pursued his career in another occupied European country, he would undoubtedly have been sentenced to death as a war criminal after the war and hanged, as were so many others who served Hitler.

Dr. Werner Best was the chief representative of the German Reich in Denmark. His official title was Reich Commissioner. He was a cynic who neither hated nor loved the Jews. If it suited his purposes, they would die. If the opposite was the case, and it promoted his career, they could survive. It suited Best that the Danish Jews should enjoy preferential treatment, compared to Jews in the rest of occupied Europe. He feared that if he let the Danish Jews be arrested and deported, the Danish people would rise up in protest. When Hitler, in September 1943, decided that Denmark was to be "Jew-free," Best was involved in a double-dealing game which resulted in his sabotage of Hitler's plan.

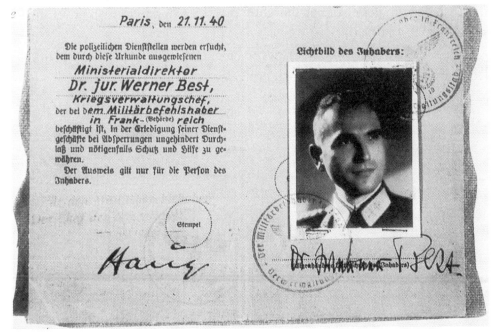

His appointment as Hitler's proxy in Denmark saved his life. Indirectly, he had the king, Christian X, to thank for this.

On September 26, 1942, the King celebrated his 72nd birthday. Hitler had sent him a fulsome congratulatory telegram. The king answered it coolly in only a few words: "Thank you very much for your congratulations, Christian Rex."

Hitler erupted in one of his notorious fits of rage. He demanded that extreme measures be taken against this presumptuous king, the government and the entire Danish population. He had very little sympathy for Denmark, the country which his foreign minister, von Ribbentrop, called "our flagship."

Denmark was their model country. It was to serve as proof that if a country behaved well under German occupation, no harm would befall its population or the country as such. Besides, Germany needed the Danish butter, pork and eggs that were being exported. These products contributed significantly to the supply of food for the German population and army.

Now Hitler would no longer tolerate that Denmark was still a largely independent country with a king, a democratically elected government and a parliament, which in many ways was independent of Germany. This had been the basis for the policy of collaboration practiced by the Danish government since April 9, 1940.

The time had come for the Danes to be punished. It was Hitler's plan that Denmark would become a German protectorate.

Doctor Werner Best was the man chosen to subjugate the Danes.

HITLER IS ENRAGED

Werner Best was highly qualified for the job. In 1931, two years before Hitler came to power in Germany, Best wrote an action plan for the Nazis. In it he described how they were to defend themselves against hostile activities.

Communists and Social Democrats were to be arrested and re-educated in concentration camps. Jews were to be unprotected by law. They would not be allowed to buy flour or medicine, to use telephones or public transportation.

This was before Hitler became chancellor in 1933. A few years later, Best, who had become a lawyer, wrote an article in which he stated that genocide was legal, provided it was efficient. That is, if there were no survivors from the targeted population.

A few years later, Best was given the opportunity to put his ideas into effect. This was in 1939-40, when Germany had occupied Poland. After the war, Best was accused of having been party to the murder of at least 8,723 Jews and gypsies. As always, he managed to evade responsibility. He was very good at this, a talent which served him well during his term of service in occupied Denmark.

As already mentioned, Hitler was furious with the king. He summoned the chief of the German forces in Denmark, Hermann von Hanneken, to the Führer headquarters in Berlin. He ordered that, in future, German soldiers were to treat Denmark as enemy territory.

Adolf Hitler, dictator of the Third Reich, at the podium. He dreamed of a Europe under German domination, where all Jews were exterminated, and all Slavic-speaking peoples were reduced to second-class citizens performing slave labor for the German people. In May of 1945, 12 years after his rise to power, Germany lay in ruins, and he committed suicide in his bunker in the besieged city of Berlin.

Best was told the same when he was summoned by Hitler to be appointed as his governor in Denmark.

But Hitler also said that he was interested in negotiating with the Danish government.

So, in actual fact, Best was left to do as he pleased in Denmark after his arrival in Copenhagen on November 5, 1942. He settled into the "Rydhave" villa in the suburb of Klampenborg, where the present American ambassador to Denmark now lives.

Best's task was to see to it that the country remained calm. As long as the export of Danish agricultural products continued and Danish industry delivered supplies to the German army, no one interfered in Best's policies. After the war, Best said that he did not hear a single word from Hitler, nor from his superior, Foreign Minister von Ribbentrop, until things began to come to a head in August 1943.

Denmark was under the authority of the Foreign Ministry in Berlin. All other occupied countries were directly under Hitler's orders. This partly accounts for the preferential treatment given to Denmark. Perhaps it also came to influence the fate of the Danish Jews.

In the Treblinka Extermination Camp the Nazis Were Able to Gas and Burn 10,000 People a Day

Hitler thought that Best was too weak, not hard enough on the Danish population – especially the Danish resistance movement which had begun to grow strong in the course of 1943. In March and April, there were many acts of sabotage in Copenhagen and elsewhere. But Hitler had little time to spare for Danish concerns. He was having problems in the east, where the war against the Soviet Union was not going well. In January 1943, large German forces had to surrender to the Soviet Red Army, after the defeat at Stalingrad. The fortunes of war were beginning to turn.

While we went on with our everyday lives, Hitler's death camps were working at full speed in Poland. During these months – from the spring of 1942 to the fall of 1943 – five to six thousand Jews were shot, starved or gassed and burned every day by the German machinery of annihilation – approximately the same number as the total Jewish population Denmark.

In Treblinka, 60 kilometers from Warsaw, a total of 850,000 Jews and 21,000 gypsies were killed during the same period. Camp commandant Franz Stangel boasted that on some days the Germans managed to kill 10,000 people in the 12 gas chambers.

HANDS OFF THE JEWS

There was relatively little interference by the German occupying power in the politics of the Danish government. As long as Denmark did not pose a threat to the German war effort, this "small, ridiculous country" was left alone.

Best continued this policy. The Danish police force was functioning. The Danish army and navy were allowed to continue playing soldier. Danish freedom fighters who were caught were placed in Danish prisons. So far no one had been executed by German bullets.

The Danish Jews were protected by this policy of collaboration. Since the start of the occupation, Danish governments had made it clear to the Germans that Danish Jews were protected by Danish law.

On April 9, 1940, six days after the start of the occupation, Cecil von Renthe-Fink, the German emissary to Denmark, wrote to his superiors in Berlin:

> If we were to go any further than strictly necessary (for instance in the matter of persecuting the Jews in Denmark) it would have a paralyzing effect and cause serious disturbances...

Best respected this attitude. He was convinced that Prime Minister Erik Scavenius and his government would resign if Hitler were to demand that

Danish Jews be deported. Best had nothing against genocide, nor against the anti-Jewish policies of the Nazis, but he wanted law and order in Denmark. If the price for this was the non-deportation of Danish Jews, he was willing to pay it.

He therefore went very far to divert the attention of his superiors from us.

In a speech given in Århus at the beginning of February 1943, Best presented his political program.

Denmark held an exceptional position among the occupied countries in Europe. Germany would respect this position. Denmark was regarded as a neutral country in which German troops were stationed. This was a regrettable fact, but a military necessity. We were living on borrowed time. And so was Best.

THE "DUMB" DANES

There was a power struggle going on between Best and von Hanneken, the chief of the German occupation forces in Denmark. Which of them had more influence in Berlin and greater power in Denmark? As long as things remained calm, it was Best. But the level of sabotage increased, and so did Hitler's impatience with Best's policy of appeasement.

Best was afraid of losing control. He also feared for his career, and probably for his life as well. He had many enemies in the Third Reich. Best may have been in no doubt as to what was happening to his and Hitler's dream of establishing a Nazi millenium. He was not a fanatical idealist. He was something worse: a coldly calculating careerist. He had jumped on the Nazi bandwaggon when that had been expedient. Now that it was heading for the abyss, he wanted to secure himself. Best was not eager to sacrifice his life for Hitler.

Best was the administrator, the cynic. He despised democracy. Nevertheless, he persuaded his superiors in Berlin to let "the dumb Danes" hold an election to parliament in March 1943. This was the only free election held during the Second World War in any of the European countries occupied by the Germans.

Best did not sympathize with the Danish Jews at all. Neither did he hate us. We were merely pawns in the game, and as long as there was hope for his politics, he protected us. As late as July 1943, he traveled to Berlin and was received by the second-greatest fiend in Germany, Heinrich Himmler. Himmler issued instructions "not to do anything in relation to the Jewish question until further orders."

That summer we spent our vacation, as we had done so often before, with a fisherman's family in Sletten near Humlebæk. When we said our goodbyes after the vacation and "see you again next summer," we had no idea how soon we would revisit the family, this time as refugees.

From Collaboration to Resistance

Collaboration was a lost game from the outset. A growing portion of the Danish population wanted a direct confrontation with the German occupying power. The Danish government wanted to continue the collaboration with the Germans, in order to protect Denmark from the calamities which a break with the Germans would cause, but the support from the population for continuing this policy slowly crumbled.

At the beginning of August 1943, spontaneous general strikes broke out in a number of towns. In Odense demonstrators beat up a German officer. On August 29, the Germans declared martial law. Demonstrations were forbidden, a curfew was imposed and saboteurs were brought before German military courts. The Danish government resigned. Parliament closed down and went home. King Christian imposed house arrest on himself at Amalienborg Castle. The Danish navy sunk its ships or sailed across The Sound to Swedish harbors. Danish soldiers were interned. The German army took over, not Best.

August 29 was the turning point in the history of the Danish occupation. Caution, indecision and practical considerations had dictated the Danish policy of collaboration since April 9, 1940. Now Denmark was on its way from neutrality to resistance and a place among the allied nations fighting Nazism.

August 29 also meant that now the Danish Jews were at Hitler's mercy. There was no one to protect us after the Danish government ceased to function. There was no reason to believe that Best would continue to favor our survival.

We Sat By As If Hypnotized

We should have known that the clock had struck. Most of us did not believe what cold reason told us, but sat by as if hypnotized.

Those who tried to stir their community into taking action were hushed up. People who claimed to have heard of the horrible things happening to other Jews in Europe were accused of creating panic.

The leaders of the Jewish community suggested that we stay calm and composed. Perhaps the Germans would forget about us. Any attempts at resistance or flight to Sweden were discouraged. This would only incite the Germans.

Besides, we did not know how we would get to Sweden. At that time the resistance movement had no well-organized escape routes across The Sound. Some members of the resistance managed to get across with the assistance of fishermen. Others rowed across – some in a kayak.

Before the persecution of the Jews began on October 1, there were hardly more than 500 Danish refugees in Sweden. Most of them were military personnel who fled after August 29. There were only a few Jews.

Viewed against the background of what we know today, the passivity of the Danish Jews is incomprehensible.

The Germans had confiscated records of all the members of the Jewish community in Denmark. The had raided the Jewish community's offices on Ny Kongen Street in Copenhagen.

This ought to have been a warning signal. But the leaders of the community had more faith in reassurances from the Danish authorities than in stark reality.

THE TELEGRAM FOR HITLER

After the Danish government had resigned, the departmental heads of the ministries had taken over.

The Chief of the Foreign Ministry, Nils Svenningsen, was in almost daily contact with Werner Best. Best assured Svenningsen that the Danish Jews had nothing to fear. Svenningsen calmed the leaders of the Jewish community in Denmark: barrister of the Supreme Court, C.B. Henriques, and the acting Chief Rabbi, Marcus Melchior. Svenningsen trusted Best.

The Jews wanted to believe that this miracle would last until Hitler had lost the war and peace came. Each time Svenningsen asked Best whether there was any truth to the rumor that actions against the Jews were under way, Best denied any knowledge of it.

He was lying, of course. For on September 8, he had sent a telegram to his superior, Foreign Minister von Ribbentrop. In this telegram he recommended that it was now time to move against "the Jews and the Freemasons."

But in the same telegram Best warned of all the problems that might arise in Denmark if his German superiors were to approve of his plan of action. In short, he continued his game of double-dealing. After the war, Best claimed that he had formulated his telegram in such a way that his superior, Foreign Minister von Ribbentrop, and Hitler would refuse to accept his recommendation. During the interrogations after the war, Best also stated he had been certain that the actions against the Jews would fail.

Why then did he suggest that the Danish Jews be deported?

One can only guess. One reason may have been that he felt the ground moving under his feet. He was afraid of losing the confidence Hitler had in him and wanted to regain it by sacrificing the Danish Jews.

Another reason may have been the power struggle between Best and the German military chief in Denmark, von Hanneken.

The action against the Jews would help to consolidate Best's power. He was given police reinforcements to use in capturing us. This failed, however, but Best was allowed to keep the gendarmes in the country and used them, for instance, to fight the Danish resistance movement.

Best was afraid of the resistance movement. If he proved unable to keep it in check, Hitler would turn over his responsibilities to the German military. This would mean more power for von Hanneken and less influence for Best. Best had not forgotten how to maneuver. First, he took the initiative to start persecuting the Jews, in order to gain favor with Hitler and Himmler. He then sabotaged his own plan, partly because he feared the reaction of the Danish population. He kept his position as Hitler's governor in Denmark until the end of the war and thus saved his own life. Had he not contributed to our escape to Sweden, he would have ended up on the gallows.

Historians disagree as to who triggered the action against the Jews. Some are of the opinion that Best, by way of his telegram of September 8, was responsible. Others think that Hitler had already decided on it before Best's wire was sent off.

After the war, Best said he had received confidential information that Hitler or Himmler had already decided on the action against the Jews before he sent his telegram.

Ten days later he received confirmation of its receipt. Hitler was taking a personal interest in the matter.

Now Best was caught in his own trap. He must obey orders, follow Hitler's instructions and carry out the persecution of the Jews which he himself had promoted.

G.F. Duckwitz was the man who obstructed the Germans' plan to capture us. He was employed at the German embassy under Werner Best. Duckwitz was an old Nazi who had had second thoughts. He had

joined the German Nazi Party as early as 1932. Since he spoke Danish, he was sent to Denmark as a spy for German Intelligence. After the German occupation on April 9, 1940, Duckwitz, the spy, was hired by the German embassy as an expert in shipping. According to Best, Duckwitz was an SS-Hauptsturmführer (captain). Duckwitz's warning served him well after the war. His Nazi past was forgiven. He became German ambassador to Denmark and a respected man in Germany. Best, on the other hand, died forgotten by all in 1989.

But Best was not through with his trickery. On September 28, his orders finally arrived from Berlin. The ships that were to pick us up were already on their way to the Langelinie Quay. One of them was the "Wartheland." Best now summoned his naval attaché, G.F. Duckwitz, to a meeting and showed him the telegram from Berlin.

He knew that Duckwitz was not a loyal Nazi. He also knew that Duckwitz had good contacts with the Danish Social Democrat leaders, among others Hans Hedtoft and H.C. Hansen, both of whom eventually became prime ministers. Duckwitz immediately contacted Hedtoft. They met in Rømersgade in Copenhagen, in the building which today houses the Workers' Museum (Arbejdermuseet). This took place on Tuesday, September 28.

"YOU ARE LYING"

That same evening Hedtoft and Hansen called on Supreme Court barrister Henriques, the chairman of the Jewish community. They were accompanied by Herman Dedichen, a representative of the resistance movement. They told Henriques that the Germans had planned to take action against the Jews on the night of October 1st. Henriques did not believe them.

After the war Hedtoft wrote:

> Henriques reacted differently from what I had expected. He spoke only three words: "You are lying." It took me quite a while to persuade him to believe me. (45)

At the same time another Social Democratic politician, Emmanuel Alsing Andersen, sent his secretary to the home of Rabbi Marcus Melchior to warn the members of the Jewish community through him.

Hedtoft also contacted the different branches of the party, encouraging them to warn the Copenhagen Jews. This was how the message reached Sofus Pedersen, who sent his son Robert out on on the evening of September 29 to warn, among others, his friend David Sampolinsky.

The result was that on the night of October 1st, when the Germans came, most Danish Jews had flown the coop.

Seeking Refuge with Strangers

They sought refuge with non-Jewish friends and acquaintances or with complete strangers who opened their doors to them.

The writer Peter P. Rohde describes a scene from those days in his book, *Midt i en ismetid* (In a Time of Isms). (46)

He was a communist and had been arrested in 1941 by the Danish police and sent to the Horserød camp along with Martin Nielsen, among others. He escaped around August 29 and went into hiding at Hanne Plum's home, the Haraldsgave Estate in Bagsværd.

In the morning he stepped into the banquet hall. "I found more than a dozen people," he writes, "seated at small tables around the room – all of them of unmistakably Semitic origin."

"I realized then that the brave, warm-hearted Mrs. Plum had without hesitation opened her doors to her Jewish friends and friends of her friends. There was Hannah Adler, the head mistress of the school; there was the writer Henri Nathansen and his wife, and there was the painter and art historian Ernst Goldschmidt."

Several Germans Were Opposed to the Action Against the Jews

After the war, Best claimed to have known that the action against the Jews would fail and that he actively contributed to its failure.

The first claim is certainly a lie. The second may have been true. We have Duckwitz's word for that after the war.

Best had no way of knowing that large numbers of Danes would rise up and protect the Jews. He likewise had no way of knowing that it would be possible, in so short a time, to establish the many escape routes that emerged in the wake of the persecutions. Nor could he have known that many German soldiers would sabotage the action, either directly or through indifference and passivity.

There is no proof that the German soldiers had orders from above to turn a blind eye to the Jews' trying to escape. The two marines who were posted on Wilder Square where the "Gerda III" was moored, and the German officer in Snekkersten Harbor who told the refugee Jew, "Take it easy, I won't harm you" – they were not obeying orders, but rather disobeying them.

From the beginning, the German army and navy were opposed to the action against the Jews. In the last days of September there was much to do among the chiefs of the German occupying power in Denmark. Everyone was trying to push the responsibility for the campaign off onto the others.

That whole idea had come from Best. He has to handle this himself, declared General von Hanneken, head of the German army in Denmark.

He refused to place German troops at Best's disposal. Best complained to his superiors in Berlin. The upshot was that von Hanneken sent 50 soldiers to Langelinie Quay, where they were to guard the deportation vessel "Wartheland."

The German navy was even less enthusiastic.

But that is not all. Even the German police chiefs' behavior was different in Denmark from that in the rest of Europe.

One of them was the Gestapo Commander Rudolf Mildner. He was sent to Denmark by Heinrich Himmler to help Best organize the operation.

Mildner had experience in killing Jews. He belonged to the SS-elite. There is nothing to indicate that he ever refused to obey orders, especially when the orders came from as high up as Hitler. Mildner came to Denmark from the Auschwitz death camp. He was responsible for the extermination of thousands of Polish Jews.

At the last moment Mildner traveled to Berlin to persuade Himmler to stop the action against us. He returned with his mission unaccomplished.

Adolf Eichmann also sent reinforcements to Copenhagen. Three of Eichmann's trusted specialists in the persecution of Jews came to Copenhagen. There they were sabotaged by the German authorities. They were assigned offices in the Dagmarhus building, but had trouble getting started, because everything was moving so slowly.

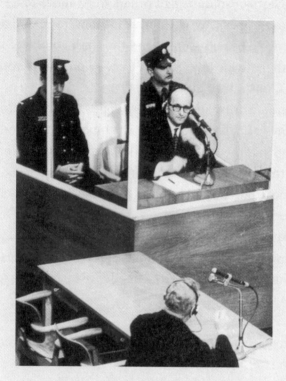

Adolf Eichmann (1906-1962). He sits in a glass cage to protect him from assassins during the trial in Jerusalem. Eichmann was sentenced to death and executed. He was the man behind the extermination of six million Jews, from 1941 to 1945.

During the trial he insisted that he was just a bureaucrat following orders. Here is an example of the power he had over human life: 10,000 Serbian Jews had been arrested and placed in concentration camps in Serbia. The German authorities were afraid that Serbian partisans would free these Jews. The Germans, however, were short of freight cars to transport them to death camps in Poland, and Eichmann was consulted to find out what to do with these 10,000 Jews. Over the phone, Eichmann answered, "Shoot them," and hung up. Thus 10,000 human beings died. After the defeat in 1945, Eichmann went underground. In 1950 he fled to Argentina. In 1960 he was captured by Israeli secret agents and carried off to Israel where he was brought to trial, accused of war crimes. He was hanged in 1962.

When the German police troops were sent into action and drove through Købmager Street and Strøget, capturing Birgit Fischermann and Salomon Katz and their families, they had been given orders that did not promote effiency.

For example, they were not allowed to smash down doors if the Jews did not open them voluntarily. They were only allowed to knock or ring the bell. If Salomon Katz had not opened his door when the four gendarmes and the Danish Nazi rang the bell, he and his family would probably not have ended up in concentration camps. One month after the failed operation, Eichmann came to Copenhagen. He was the technician behind the apparatus designed to annihilate the Jews in Europe.

At that time the Germans had already murdered 850,000 Jews in the Treblinka concentration camp. They had shot 130,000 Jews in Rombula outside of Riga in Latvia, and so on. The gas chambers had been working at full speed since the spring of 1942.

During his visit to Copenhagen, the mass murderer Eichmann negotiated with Best.

Eichmann promised Best that the 477 Danish Jews who had been deported to Theresienstadt would not be "sent east."

This was an innocent-sounding expression, but it was a euphemism for: "sent to the gas chambers." The Germans had made up a whole set of code words to cover up their genocide. To be "sent east" was one of them. Many Jews let themselves be reassured by the expression. They thought it just meant that they were to be slave laborers in the camps in Poland. When they discovered the truth, it was too late.

Best was also given other promises by Eichmann. Representatives of the Danish Red Cross would soon be permitted to visit the Danish prisoners in Theresienstadt, who would also be allowed to receive packages of food. Five Danes, who had been deported to Theresienstadt, were sent home again because they were either married to non-Jews or were only partly Jewish. Best sought to limit the harm he had done, and Eichmann gave in. This was the same Eichmann who one year later would organize the murder of 600,000 Hungarian Jews.

BEST SAVES HIS OWN LIFE

Denmark was still an exceptional case, seen from Best's point of view, and the Danish Jews in Theresienstadt were therefore given preferential treatment.

Werner Best is led away from Dagmar House which served as German headquarters in Copenhagen during the occupation. In the middle, a freedom fighter, recognizable by his armband. Best is on the right.

Best thought he could put a damper on the Danish population's will to resist and their anger at the terrible events which his telegram to Hitler of September 8 had caused.

Perhaps he also thought of ensuring his own safety after the defeat of the Nazis, which was now only a matter of time.

He knew that he would be brought before a Danish court after the occupation, accused of war crimes. He tried to build up some goodwill for himself. It might save his life. Best had always feared situations where he could not evade responsibility.

He now played his greatest double-dealing game ever. And it succeeded. He got away with his crimes in Poland, Czechoslovakia, France and Denmark during the occupation with both his life and his freedom intact, after spending only a short time in prison.

One can only guess at the reasons for this. One would assume that Best's warning to Duckwitz about the planned persecution of the Jews, and his attempts to ameliorate the predicament of the Jewish prisoners in Theresienstadt, contributed to the mildness of his sentence.

In April 1966, Johan Hvidtfeldt, who was then Keeper of the Public Records, said in an interview with the newspaper *Information*:

> The more you study Best and his deeds during the occupation, the less damaging evidence you find. Today you can find evidence that in several cases he contradicted his superiors. He contradicted the SS, and his relationship with the Wehrmacht was extraordinarily tense.

Best was sentenced to death at the Copenhagen city court in 1948.

In 1949 his sentence was reduced to five years in prison.

In 1950 the Supreme Court ordered him incarcerated for 12 years.

In 1951 he was expelled from Denmark.

The date was August 29 – not the best date to choose to return the "Bloodhound of Paris" to freedom.

In November 1960, Duckwitz was honored at a reception at the Danish embassy in Bonn. This took place in connection with the publication of the German translation of Åge Bertelsen's book *Oktober '43*. Bertelsen played an important part in the extrication of the Jews. His rescue organization, the Lyngby-group, brought about 1,000 Jews to safety in Sweden.

After the ceremony Duckwitz wrote a letter to Best who, after his release, had settled in the town of Mühlheim in the Ruhr district of Germany.

In his letter Duckwitz tells his former boss that in his speech he had mentioned that "you did what was in your power to enable as many Jews as possible to go to Sweden." (47)

In another context Duckwitz cited Best as having wished that it were "possible to build a bridge across The Sound, so that the Danish Jews could get to safety in Sweden." (48)

After his release Best worked as a lawyer for his old friends in the SS. He was one of the few high-ranking Nazis to survive both the war and the war crimes trials. At every opportunity Duckwitz stated that it was Best who had issued the warning which saved the Danish Jews.

We Did Not Know Until Later

We were lucky. Our passage across was almost untroubled, except for the time when the engine stopped in the middle of The Sound, but by then we were already safe.

Others were on the run for ten days or more before they succeeded in getting across. One family, for example, had to flee from Lyngby to the North Harbor, from there to Lillerød, then back to Copenhagen, by train to Gilleleje, back to Copenhagen, and then to Køge, before they finally managed to get across.

We were rushing around like blind mice, afraid of getting caught while sleeping at the houses of friends or strangers, afraid when riding in a hired car or on the train.

Neither we nor our helpers had any way of knowing that the danger was limited, due to the fact that the Germans were not making the greatest possible effort to arrest us.

We all thought that our lives were at stake every hour of the day.

We could not know, for instance, that Camman, the German harbor commandant in Copenhagen, was a friend of Duckwitz. He had ordered the German coast guard boats to be sent to the shipyard for repairs during just those critical days.

Neither could we know that the German Wehrmacht refused to participate in the persecution of the Jews. And John Saietz's father had no way of knowing that a German officer would reassure him that night when they accidentally met in the Snekkersten Harbor.

We had no way of knowing that King Christian X would have the courage to protest against the persecution of the Jews in a letter delivered to Best on October 1 at 6:50 p.m. The police action taken against us began that same night at 9:10 p.m. In his letter of protest the king warns against the consequences of any action taken against the Danish Jews. In his telegram to Berlin regarding the king's protest, Best predicted that the operation would fail. This he could safely state, since he himself had warned the Danish Jews through Duckwitz several days before.

We could not know that Copenhagen's bishop, Hans Fuglsang-Damgaard, would send a pastoral letter to all the priests in the country, which they were to read aloud in church to protest the persecution.

And we had no way of knowing that there would be girls like the two Lund sisters, or Karen-Lykke Poulsen, or Henny Sinding Sundø, or Elsebeth Kieler, who dared run the risk and help us to safety.

Not to mention all the others, the doctors and nurses in the Copenhagen hospitals, the coast guards, the ambulance drivers and the fishermen and their wives. Or Karen from Sæby who was pregnant but had the strength to say to her husband, "Of course you must take those who need it across."

On September 13, 1943, Duckwitz wrote in his diary:

"I know what I must do."

Duckwitz's decision to do what he thought was right could have meant the signing of his own death warrant.

He opposed what was considered most sacred in the Third Reich: an order from the Führer, an edict from Adolf Hitler.

Only a few dared do so. And almost none did it and survived.

If Best's plan to warn the Jews had been revealed, Duckwitz would have been convicted as a traitor. Best would perhaps have made it; he was an expert in survival.

THE EXCEPTION

We stayed in Sweden for 19 months. We went to Danish schools in Göteborg and Lund. The teachers were fugitives like the rest of us. The schoolbooks had been smuggled across The Sound on the Danish-Swedish Refugee Service's boats, that is to say, when they had room for something other than saboteurs and allied pilots who had been shot down over Denmark and had to reach safety. We took the same exams as our contemporaries in Denmark.

The German defeat was only a matter of time. At home the resistance against the Germans grew. Some of the expatriate students in the higher classes lost patience with living as refugees and went across The Sound illegally to continue working in the resistance movement.

The Danish Brigade

It was hard for us in the first year of the gymnasium to accept that we were too young to enlist in the Danish Brigade. The Brigade had been established to intervene if the Germans in Denmark refused to surrender voluntarily. You had to be 18 to be a member of the Brigade. After prolonged negotiations and threats of strikes among the students at the Danish schools, the Commanding Officer of the Brigade agreed to disregard the minimum age limit and accepted us on equal terms with our older friends.

The Danish Brigade comes to Copenhagen on May 6, 1945. We were cheered as the victors of the war, but the truth was that we hadn't fired a single shot to free Denmark because the Germans surrendered. The Brigade consisted of 4,790 men.

On May 5, 1945, on the Danish News broadcast by the BBC, it was announced that "German forces in Northwest Germany and Denmark have surrendered."

Our homecoming on the ferry from Helsingborg to Copenhagen via Helsingør became a triumphal procession.

There was no fighting. Only on Jagtvej in Copenhagen and near Vesterport station, some Danes in German service shot at us from the rooftops. The only shot I fired while serving in the Brigade was accidental and nearly cost my best friend his life.

The Germans Did Not Want to Open a New Front in Denmark

The occupation ended as it had begun: without major combat, without destruction.

Denmark emerged from the five years of world war practically unharmed when compared to other European countries.

The Soviet Union lost more than 17 million people, civilians and soldiers. Germany lost 5.5 million, Great Britain 460,000 and the USA 300,000. American losses included only soldiers, because the war did not reach the USA and therefore did not affect civilians. The Jews lost more than 6 million people and Denmark lost 4,800. These casualties did not include Danes who were in German service during the war. Their number is unknown.

Danish sailors in the service of the Allies during the war suffered the worst casualties: 1,886. This number includes a few fishermen.

Six hundred three Danes died in German prisons and concentration camps. Fifty-four of them were Jews who had been deported to Theresienstadt – a little over 10% of the Danish Jews captured by the Germans during the persecution. They died from sickness and old age.

The mass murderer Adolf Eichmann kept the promise he gave to Best during his visit to Copenhagen in early November 1943. The Danish Jews were not deported from Theresienstadt to extermination camps. German organization and bureaucracy worked.

Thus a Dane, who was a child in Theresienstadt, recounts that he was placed in a so-called hospital barrack for children. His parents came to visit him in the barrack, where they found him crawling around on the floor all by himself. All the other children, as well as the doctors and nurses, had been sent to the death camps, where they were gassed. This Danish child was the only exception.

320 died as a result of air raids.

103 resistance fighters were shot by the Germans in Ryvangen after being sentenced to death.

900 were killed by the Germans or their Danish henchmen in revenge for actions carried out by the resistance.

670 Danes were killed during spontaneous general strikes and acts of sabotage.

And 71 Danish volunteer soldiers fell in the Allied armies. (49)

The remaining 240 were civilians and soldiers who lost their lives on the four most decisive days of the war:

April 9, 1940, when Denmark was occupied.

August 29, 1943, when the Danish population broke with the policy of collaboration with Germany.

September 19, 1944, when the Germans arrested the Danish police force and deported them to the Neuengamme concentration camp in Germany.

And on or about May 4, 1945 – Liberation Day.

THE HOMECOMING

The civilian Danish refugees returned home in the weeks following the liberation. Along with them came the survivors from Theresienstadt.

On April 14, they had been picked up by Swedish Count Bernadotte's white busses, which drove them straight through devastated Germany to Sweden.

And on May 6, the Jews in Copenhagen held a celebration service in the synagogue on Krystal Street.

They continued where they had left off on September 29, 1943, when Rabbi Marcus Melchior had interrupted the service to tell them to flee.

A Meaning in Life

My military career in the Danish Brigade ended in Frøslev, the camp in which the fisherman from Sæby and his friends had been prisoners, punished for sailing refugees across the Kattegat to Sweden.

Our job was to escort the German soldiers home across the border.

They came walking, by the thousands, day after day, with their heads bowed down. They had discarded their weapons and helmets in ditches along the highways. The sick were transported on trucks or on horse-drawn carts.

Some were dragging food supplies which they were hoping to bring home with them.

Most German towns were in ruins. There was hunger in the streets. It was an army of ragamuffins who dragged themselves home through the Danish spring landscape.

I remembered them as they had come on April 9, 1940: powerful, with shiny weapons, confident of victory after having brought all of Europe under their heel. They came marching across the Langelinie Bridge, down toward Østerport station, on their way to the Nyboder school, which had been requisitioned as a German barracks.

"Wir fahren gegen Engeland," they were singing. And "Die Fahne hoch." Above our heads the black Stuka-planes howling. They dove down over the roofs of Copenhagen to convince us that resistance was impossible.

Rabbi Max Friediger, religious leader of the Danish Jews, returns home on May 28, 1945. He had been arrested by the Germans along with other prominent Danes on August 29, 1943, placed in the Horserød camp and from there sent to Theresienstadt.

Now they were shuffling home across the border. And we had our fun with them.

The last kilometer they were allowed to choose whether they wanted to run home, or goose-step as they had done when they came.

This was not very considerate, but we were young and feeling victorious. We had not fired a single shot in combat. The Germans had surrendered and cheated us out of a war. Now at least they had to be humiliated.

Since then I have often thought of this victorious attitude in shame. For it was not we who had won the war. It had been won by the allied soldiers and the European resistance movements. We merely came to sweep up afterwards.

One day I was invited to speak in Sankelmark at the annual meeting of the German minority in Denmark, which numbers about 15,000 people.

I talked about the choice we had given the German soldiers. Most of them preferred to run home across the border. The whole thing was meaningless.

After the speech a man came up to me. He was my own age.

"I was one of the people you talked about," he said. "I chose to run across the border. I had had enough of goose-stepping. I want to thank you. Ever since the war I have wondered what it meant that we had to choose. I have wondered and wondered. Now I know that it had no meaning. Now maybe I can forget."

We cannot help looking for meaning in life.

Sometimes it is hopeless, sometimes we succeed.

If we are able to learn from our experiences, if we come to understand a little more about life, that is, about ourselves and our fellow men, then even tragic events like the ones we experienced during the occupation can have some meaning.

The thousands and thousands who helped us reach safety behaved in a way that is hard to define in words. Solidarity, humane behavior, love of one's fellows. These are such big words that they lose credibility. They are so bombastic, and that was just what it was not. The rescue operation was anonymous; it went on quietly and unspectacularly. There were no generals or privates. People did what was needed. As Duckwitz wrote in his diary, "I know what I must do."

Returning to Everyday Life

People were torn out of their everyday existence, and after the job was done, most of them returned to wherever they had come from. They received no medals or parades. Most remained unsung heroes. Some are being revealed for the first time in this account of the events.

Many Jews did not know whom to thank for their lives when they returned from Sweden.

Who was the girl with the red beret and the young man who ran through the streets of Copenhagen to warn Jews who thought they had nothing to fear?

Now we know that one of them was a student named Ebba Lund and the other an apprenticed typographer named Robert Pedersen.

A Jewish State

After finishing secondary school, I signed up as a volunteer in the Jewish resistance movement, Haganah.

The movement was fighting to establish a Jewish state in Palestine.

The Germans had killed six million Jews during the Second World War. A million and a half of them were children.

It was not the first time in history that Jews had been killed because they were Jews. It must not happen again.

The solution was for the Jews to have their own state, to become a nation like others, with a country of their own. This could not happen without a fight, and Haganah was preparing for this. I enlisted along with 35 other Danes. Most of them were former members of the Brigade. This was my way of finding some meaning in what I had experienced during the war and the occupation.

You CAN Do Something!

Before the German occupation of Denmark there was a what's-the-use atmosphere in Denmark. After all, we would not be able to stand up against our strong neighbor to the south.

It was not my last war. In March of 1948, a group of young Danish Jews volunteered for the Jewish resistance movement, the Haganah (Defense) in Palestine.

The conflict in Palestine developed into a full-scale war between the Jews and the Arab countries. The State of Israel was proclaimed on May 14, 1948. The Arab attack began the same day. About 35 young Danes fought for Israel as volunteer soldiers. Three were wounded, none killed. I chose to settle in Israel in 1954, and I live there with my family today. The photograph was taken in Tel Aviv during a short cease-fire between battles in 1948.

The resistance movement and the rescue of the Danish Jews shows that often you CAN do something. People can accomplish something – even fighting against a superior power – if only they dare make a choice.

There is an old Jewish saying that he who saves the life of one man has saved a whole world. That sounds reasonable, and it is worth trying to live up to.

That was what many Danes did 50 years ago.

THE KISS

This story is about a kiss. It was given 50 years ago in an ambulance going on a dangerous journey from Helsingør Hospital to a hospital in Copenhagen. It was a one-way kiss, not an exchange of kisses. The recipient was lying half unconscious on a stretcher, hit in the stomach by a German dum-dum bullet.

This story is also about a lot of other things that went on at that time and can only be described if one dares use words which today would call forth condescending smiles at best – words such as personal courage, self-sacrifice, decency.

It is a story of a group of young people who during the occupation felt morally obligated to help fellow beings in mortal danger. They did not take refuge in a what's-the-use attitude. Instead of looking for reasons for passivity, they just acted.

"Of course we were afraid," said one of them at a modest memorial ceremony at the Helsingør City Hall, "but the anger was greater than the fear." His name was Børge Rønne. The man on the stretcher is named Thormod Larsen, and the woman who kissed him was Tove Wandborg.

The group used the cover name of The Helsingør Sewing Circle. Recently its members were honored at a ceremony in Washington, D.C., where the contributions made by them and other Danish resistance members were praised by President Clinton. The most active member of The Sewing Circle,

Thormod Larsen, 86, and Tove Wandborg, 82, on the beach near Hellebæk where German bullets had brought him down in 1944. Tove Wandborg, at the time a nurse at Elsinore Hospital, saved his life.

Erling Kiær, died in 1980, partly as a result of the damage his health suffered when he was caught by the Germans in May 1944, and sent to a concentration camp. (50)

Kiær was a bookbinder by profession. He had served as a lieutenant in the army and could drive a tractor. When he started his career as the "Pimpernel of The Sound," he had no experience with either boats or the sea. His daring and a large supply of sea-sickness pills were his most important allies. He was active for two years; before the Germans got him, Kiær sailed more than 1,400 people across The Sound. Half of them were Jews who had to escape in October and November of 1943, and the other half were freedom fighters who had to be brought to safety in Sweden. Kiær had his permanent base in Helsingborg. Often he would cross The Sound two or three times in a row, especially during the long winter nights. He was an expert at getting out of German traps – until that night in May when his boat was surrounded by five or six patrol boats. A bullet hit his engine and his fate was sealed.

Thormod Larsen, then a detective inspector, was one of Kiær's assistants on shore. He was seized by the Germans in January 1944.

It was on a lightly overcast night. Rønne remembers that he was feeling strangely uneasy. "Even today I cannot explain why," he says. "It was an intuitive feeling of premonition, hard to define."

Kiær was supposed to meet them at 11 p.m. on the northern beach of Hellebæk. The refugees were waiting and Kiær's boat approached the coast. They had started to embark, when a German patrol coming from the Coastal Road detected them. Bullets went flying, but Kiær got away with his cargo of refugees. Thormod Larsen lay on the beach. A German bullet had penetrated his abdomen. On its way out the bullet left a ten-centimeter-wide wound. He was taken to the Helsingør Hospital, and from there he was brought by ambulance to Copenhagen, accompanied by a nurse. As the ambulance was leaving by the back gate, the Germans came rushing through the front gate to arrest Thormod Larsen.

"Do you remember the trip?" asks Tove Wandborg, 50 years later. "I was practically unconscious from the loss of blood," replies Thormod.

"You were thirsty, you called out for water," says Tove Wandborg. "But there wasn't any in the ambulance."

Thormod nods. He has heard the story before. The survivors of the group meet several times a year and refresh their memories of the old stories.

"Now I'll tell you something which you've never heard before," continues Tove Wandborg. There is a gleam in her eye. Thormod bends forward, perhaps his hearing is beginning to fail. He is 86 years old, she is 82.

"I had to do something to alleviate your thirst," she says. "So I gathered some spittle in my mouth. Then I bent down over you and gave you a kiss."

"You did not," protests Thormod and blushes profoundly.

"Yes I did," she reiterates.

Thormod starts coughing. He is gasping slightly for breath.

"Just relax Thormod," she says, "and you'll be all right." She looks at him tenderly.

That was the story of a kiss, told 50 years later. "When we die, we leave behind what surrounded us," a wise man said to me recently. "Let that be a comfort to us."

Perhaps he is right. But we do not leave behind our stories; not unless they are told and remembered. If it had not been for that conversation on the beach north of Hellebæk, 50 years later, at the place where Thormod Larsen was shot, the story of this kiss would have been forgotten.

And posterity would be the poorer.

List of Sources

1. Ugeskrift for Retsvæsen (Weekly Judicial Publication) 1950, p.453.
2. Erling Foss, as quoted in Leni Yahil's book, *Et Demokrati på prøve. Jøderne i Danmark under besættelsen* (A Democracy Put to the Test: The Jews in Denmark During the Occupation) pp. 168-169. Gyldendal 1966.
3. Jørgen Kieler's archives.
4. Valdemar Koppel in an essay in *Politiken* titled *"Dansk jøde med Gestapo i hælene"* (A Danish Jew with Gestapo at his Heels), reprinted October 2nd, 1983.
5. Robert Pedersen's account. The author's archives.
6. Told to Ella Juul Kjærulf.
7. Leni Yahil, p. 196 (see note 2).
8. Ole Lippmann's account. The author's archives.
9. Halfdan Rasmussen (born 1915): *Digte under besættelsen* (Poems From the Occupation). Carit Andersen's Forlag 1945.
10. Eye specialist Steffen Lund: *Den Hvide Brigade. Danske lægers modstand* (The White Brigade: The Resistance of Danish Physicians) pp. 175-202. Carl Allers Bogforlag.
11. Jørgen Gersfelt: *Sådan narrede vi Gestapo* (How We Cheated the Gestapo). Gyldendal 1945.
12. Otto Gelsted (1888-1968): *Emigrantdigte* (Emigrant Poems). Athenæum 1945. Gelsted calls one of the deportation ships Vaterland, its real name was Wartheland.
13. Johannes Christiansen: *"Hemmelig Vej til Palæstina"* (A Secret Path to Palestine). The weekly magazine *Familie-Journalen*, nos. 36 and 37, 1963.
14. Uri Yaari (alias Hermann Waldmann): *Konfrontationer* (Confrontations). Munksgård 1980.
15. Erik Østerholm's account. The author's archives.
16. Torben L. Meyer: *Flugten over Øresund* (The Flight Across The Sound). Jespersen & Pio's Forlag 1945.
17. Ralph Oppenhejm: *Det skulle så være* (It Came to Pass). Carit Andersen's Forlag 1966.
18. Birgit Fischermann, in an interview with Sanne Stitz at the Munkegaard School, Copenhagen 1991. The author's archives.
19. Johan Grün's account. The author's archives.

176 IN DENMARK IT COULD NOT HAPPEN

20. Jørgen Kieler: *Nordens lænkehunde. Den første Holger Danske Gruppe* (The Scandinavian Watchdogs: The First Holger Danske Group). Gyldendal 1993.
21. Salomon Katz: *Dagbog fra Theresienstadt* (A Theresienstadt Diary). Published by Hans Sode-Madsen.
22. Martin Nielsen: *Danske i tyske koncentrationslejre* (Danes in German Concentration Camps). Gyldendal 1945.
23. Ole Helweg: *Rødderne rådner* (Rotting Roots). Gyldendal 1945.
24. *Den åbne dør til den frie verden. Dansk-Svensk Flygtningetjeneste fra Malmø* (The Door to the Free World: The Danish-Swedish Refugee Service). Private edition 1945.
25. Karen-Lykke Poulsen's account. The author's archives.
26. Ulf Ekman's account. The author's archives.
27. Karen-Lykke Poulsen's account.
28. *En modstandsgruppes historie* (The Story of a Resistance Group) I and II. Written by members of the Frit Danmark student group and the Holger Danske group. Edited by Jørgen Kieler, 1982.
29. Henny Sinding Sundø's account. The author's archives.
30. Sam Besekow's account. The author's archives.
31. Anders Bjørnvad: *Hjemmehæren* (The Home Army), Odense 1988.
32. Kalle Moss: *En fiskerdrengs oplevelser på godt og ondt* (The Experiences of a Ship's Boy). Private edition. Sæby 1989.
33. Erik Stenersen's account to Bob Ramsing. The author's archives.
34. Kaj Christiansen's account to Bob Ramsing. The author's archives.
35. John Saietz's account. The author's archives.
36. Leo Igelski's account. The author's archives.
37. Account by Jørgen Glenthøj based on a statement by the German priest and historian Rudolf Wentorf. The author's archives.
38. Erik Hoffmann, Friedrich-Wilhelm Lübke, in *Der Landskreis Flensburg*, 1991.
39. Fact related by Louis Beilin. The author's archives.
40. Lillian Melchior. Told to the author.
41. *Konflikt og samarbejde* (Conflict and Cooperation). Volume in Homage to Carl-Axel Gemzell. Ed. Hans Kirchhof, Copenhagen University 1993.
42. Hans Hedtoft in Åge Bertelsen's book *Oktober '43*. Gyldendal 1993.
43. Peter P. Rohde: *Midt i en Ismetid* (In a time of Isms). Gyldendal 1970.
44. Rasmus Kreth and Michael B. Mogensen: *"Aktionen mod de danske jøder i oktober 1943 med særligt henblik på de danske og tyske myndigheders ageren"* (The Action Taken Against the Danish Jews in October 1943, with Special Reference to the Conduct of the Danish and German Authorities). Thesis published by the History Institute at Århus University, 1994.
45. S. Matlok: *Danmark i Hitlers hånd* (Denmark in Hitler's Hand), p. 125. Holkenfeldt's Forlag 1989.
46. Fact supplied by The Resistance Museum.
47. Børge Rønne: *"Helsingør Syklub"* (The Helsingør Sewing Circle). In the annual publication by the Helsingør Town Museum, 1980.